UNDERSTANDING AND USING
ENGLISH GRAMMAR

Second Edition

WORKBOOK Volume A

Betty Schrampfer Azar
Donald A. Azar

Chief contributor: Rachel Spack Koch
Contributors: Susan Jamieson
Barbara Andrews
Jeanie Francis

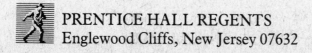

PRENTICE HALL REGENTS
Englewood Cliffs, New Jersey 07632

Editorial/production supervision: *Janet Johnston*
Interior design: *Ros Herion Freese*
Illustrations: *Don Martinetti*
Cover design: *Joel Mitnick Design*
Manufacturing buyer: *Ray Keating*

Printed in the United States of America

10 9 8 7 6 5 4 3 2 1

ISBN 0-13-943986-2

Prentice-Hall International (UK) Limited, *London*
Prentice-Hall of Australia Pty. Limited, *Sydney*
Prentice-Hall Canada Inc., *Toronto*
Prentice-Hall Hispanoamericana, S.A., *Mexico*
Prentice-Hall of India Private Limited, *New Delhi*
Prentice-Hall of Japan, Inc., *Tokyo*
Simon & Schuster Asia Pte. Ltd., *Singapore*
Editora Prentice-Hall do Brasil, Ltda., *Rio de Janeiro*

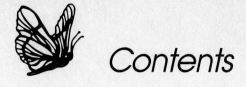

Contents

Chapter 2 MODAL AUXILIARIES AND SIMILAR EXPRESSIONS 43

Chapter 3 THE PASSIVE 74

Preface

This ESL grammar workbook accompanies *Understanding and Using English Grammar (Second Edition)*. It is a place for students to explore and practice structures on their own. At the same time, the workbook provides supplementary teaching materials for the teacher to select as needed. The exercises are designated (1) SELFSTUDY PRACTICES or (2) GUIDED STUDY PRACTICES:

(1) The SELFSTUDY PRACTICES are designed for independent out-of-class use by the students, who can correct their own work by referring to the Answer Key Booklet at the back of the workbook. The SELFSTUDY PRACTICES allow students ample opportunities to clarify their understandings, explore structures at their own pace, assess their proficiency, and expand their usage ability as well as their vocabulary.

(2) The GUIDED STUDY PRACTICES, for which the answers are not given, are intended primarily as additional material for the teacher to use as s/he sees the need. They can be used for classwork, homework, or individualized instruction.

The content of the exercises often seeks to inform, challenge, and pique the curiosity of students as they practice their English language skills. In addition, the workbook contains suggestions for various language-learning activities such as discussions, games, and writing topics.

There are two workbooks. *Workbook Volume A* has exercises for Chapters 1–4 and Appendix 1. *Workbook Volume B* contains exercises for Chapters 5–10. The workbooks are coordinated with the main text. The heading for each practice refers the students to the charts in the main text that contain explanations of the grammar being practiced. The *Teacher's Guide* that accompanies the main text includes suggestions for using the workbooks, plus answers to the GUIDED STUDY PRACTICES.

The answer key to the SELFSTUDY PRACTICES is on perforated pages. The students can remove it to construct their own separate Answer Key Booklet. The students can write in the workbook and then place the Answer Key Booklet next to the workbook to make it easy for them to correct their answers.

ACKNOWLEDGMENTS

My thanks go to all who have made this project possible. First of all to Don, an experienced ESL teacher and administrator, who at my urging turned his hand to writing. The enjoyment he took in his task is evident in the lively spirit of the workbook.

I also thank the contributors—Shelley Koch, Susan Jamieson, Jeanie Francis, and Barbara Andrews—for the wonderful materials they provided us to work with. They are experienced teachers who understand their students. Their understandings have greatly enhanced the workbook.

My mom and dad are also due great thanks. My mom keyboards and holds me to account for every word and punctuation mark, and my dad contributes a plethora of ideas for contexts. My thanks also to Chelsea for her help in the office and to Joy Edwards for her able and valued assistance.

And, of course, no book is possible without thoughtful editors: thanks go to Tina Carver, Ros Herion, Sylvia Moore, Janet Johnston—and all the support circle at Prentice Hall Regents.

BETTY S. AZAR
Langley, Washington

First, foremost, and above all, I want to express my appreciation to Betty. Although we worked together teaching ESL for many years, collaboration on this writing project brought our work lives together in a very different way. Her patience, her guidance, and her incredible expertise kept me from roaming too far afield from our objective. She taught me a great deal.

I also want to express my gratitude to our contributing writers: Rachel Spack (Shelley) Koch, Susan Jamieson, Barbara Andrews, and Jeanie Francis. They worked with me in developing draft material and did their part well. I also thank them for adapting to any inconsistencies in communications and schedule.

And finally, there's Chelsea Parker. She went through it all with us, and she'll have to do it again. Our work, and we, are all the better for that.

DONALD A. AZAR
Langley, Washington

This book is dedicated
to Chelsea
with all our love.

CHAPTER 1
Verb Tenses

◇ **PRACTICE 1—SELFSTUDY: Verb tenses. (Charts 1-1 → 1-5)**

Directions: Following are some dialogues between Speaker A and Speaker B. Complete the dialogues by using the correct form of the words in parentheses.

1. A: I'm going to ask you some questions so that we can practice verb tenses. Okay?

    B: Okay.

    A: What (*you, do*) _____ **do you do** _____ every day before you come to class? Name one thing.

    B: I (*eat*) _____ **eat** _____ breakfast.

2. A: What (*you, do*) _____ last night? Name three separate activities.

    B: Last night I (*eat*) _____ dinner. Then I (*visit*) _____ some friends, and later I (*write*) _____ a couple of letters.

3. A: What (*you, do*) _____ right now? What activity is in progress right now, at this exact moment?

    B: Right now I (*talk*) _____ to you. I (*answer*) _____ your questions.

4. A: Where were you at this exact time yesterday? And what activity was in progress yesterday at that time?

    B: Let me think. At this exact time yesterday, I was at the bookstore. I (*look*) _____ _____ for the books I needed to buy for this class.

5. A: How many questions (*I, ask*) _____ since we began this exercise?

    B: I don't know exactly. I think you (*ask*) _____ me about five or six questions since we began this exercise.

6. A: What (you, do) _____ for the past five minutes? In other words, what activity began five minutes ago and has been in progress from that time to the present time?

   B: I (talk) _____ to you for the past five minutes. I started talking to you five minutes ago, and I am still talking to you.

7. A: Where (you, be) _____ tomorrow morning?

   B: I (be) _____ in class tomorrow morning.

8. A: What (you, do) _____ at this exact time tomorrow? In other words, what activity will be in progress at this exact same time tomorrow?

   B: Right now I am sitting in the classroom. And at this exact time tomorrow, I (sit) _____ in the classroom.

9. A: What (you, do) _____ by the time you got to class today? In other words, what is one activity that you had completed before you arrived in class today?

   B: Well, for one thing, I (eat) _____ breakfast by the time I got to class today.

10. A: What (you, do) _____ by the time you go to bed tonight? Name one activity that you will have completed before you go to bed tonight.

    B: I (eat) _____ dinner by the time I go to bed tonight.

    A: Excellent! You have a good start on understanding and using English verb tenses. In this chapter, we'll do a lot more practice with all the tenses.

◇ PRACTICE 2—SELFSTUDY: Names of verb tenses. (Charts 1-1 → 1-5)

Directions: In the following dialogues, many of the verbs are in italics. Using the list of English verb tenses, write the names of the tenses of the italicized verbs.*

✔ simple present   present progressive   present perfect   present perfect progressive
  simple past   past progressive   past perfect   past perfect progressive
  simple future   future progressive   future perfect   future perfect progressive

1. A: What *do you do* every morning?

   B: I *catch* a bus to school.

   _____ **simple present** _____

2. A: What *did you do* last night?

   B: Last night I *watched* a movie on television.

   _____

_____

*Words that are "italized" or "in italics" have a slanted print. For example:
  Regular print looks like this. *Italic print looks like this.*

3. A: What *are you doing* right now?

   B: Right now I *am working* on English grammar.

   _____

4. A: What *were you doing* at this time yesterday?

   B: At this exact time yesterday, I *was walking* from the bookstore to the classroom building.

   _____

5. A: *Have you met* many people since you came here?

   B: Yes, *I've met* a lot of people.

   _____

6. A: What *have you been doing* for the past few minutes?

   B: *I have been working on* this grammar practice.

   _____

7. A: What *will you do* if you miss the bus tomorrow morning?

   B: *I'll walk* to school.

   _____

8. A: What *will you be doing* at this exact moment tomorrow?

   B: I *will be attending* my English class at this same time tomorrow.

   _____

9. A: What *had you done* by the time you got to class today?

   B: I *had bought* two books at the bookstore.

   _____

10. A: What *will you have done* by the time you go to bed tonight?

    B: I *will have finished* my homework.

    _____

11. A: Were you asleep when your friend called last night?

    B: Yes. I *had been sleeping* for almost an hour when the phone rang.

    _____

12. A: How long have you been working in this workbook?

    B: By the time I finish this practice, *I will have been working* on this grammar for ten minutes.

    _____

◇ **PRACTICE 3—SELFSTUDY: Verb tenses. (Charts 1-1 → 1-5)**

Directions: Complete the sentences with the correct form of the words in parentheses.

SIMPLE	PROGRESSIVE

PRESENT

1. Tom has regular habits. He (*eat*) _____ dinner every day. He has eaten dinner every day since he was a child. He ate dinner every day last month. He ate dinner yesterday. He will eat dinner tomorrow. He will probably eat dinner almost every day until the end of his life.

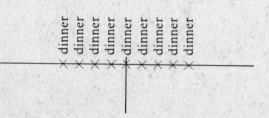

4. At 7:00 this evening, Tom started to eat dinner. It is now 7:15. Tom is on the phone because Mary called him. He says, "Can I call you back? I (*eat*) _____ dinner right now. I'll finish soon and will call you back. I don't want my dinner to get cold." Tom's dinner is in progress when Mary calls.

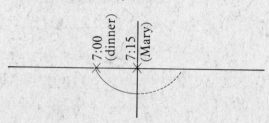

PAST

2. Tom eats dinner every day. Usually he eats at home, but yesterday he (*eat*) _____ dinner at a restaurant.

5. Last week Tom went to a restaurant. He began to eat at 7:00. At 7:15 Mary came into the restaurant, saw Tom, and walked over to say hello. Tom's dinner was still in front of him. He hadn't finished it yet. In other words, when Mary walked into the restaurant, Tom (*eat*) _____ dinner. Tom's dinner was in progress when Mary arrived.

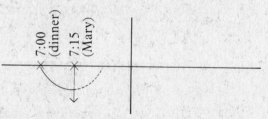

FUTURE

3. Tom ate dinner yesterday. He eats dinner every day. In all probability, he (*eat*) _____ dinner tomorrow.

6. Tom will begin his dinner at 7:00 tonight. Mary will arrive at 7:15. It takes Tom 30 minutes to eat his dinner. In other words, when Mary arrives tonight, Tom (*eat*) _____ his dinner. Tom's dinner will be in progress when Mary arrives.

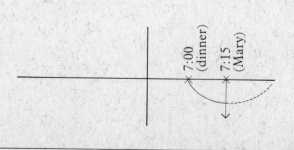

PERFECT	**PERFECT PROGRESSIVE**

7. Tom finished eating dinner at 7:30 tonight. It is now 8:00, and his mother has just come into the kitchen. She says, "What would you like for dinner? Could I cook something for you?" Tom says, "Thanks Mom, but I (*eat, already*)

_____ dinner."

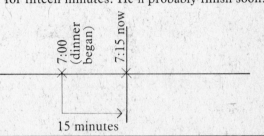

10. Tom began to eat dinner at 7:00 tonight. It is now, at this moment, 7:15. Tom (*eat*)

_____ his dinner for fifteen minutes, but he hasn't finished yet. In other words, his dinner has been in progress for fifteen minutes. He'll probably finish soon.

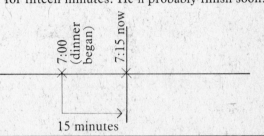

8. Yesterday Tom cooked his own dinner. He began to eat at 7:00 and finished at 7:30. At 8:00 his mother came into the kitchen. She offered to cook some food for Tom, but he (*eat, already*)

_____. In other words, Tom had finished his dinner before he talked to his mother.

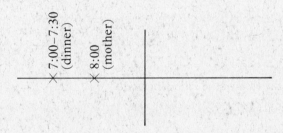

11. Last week Tom went to a restaurant. He began to eat at 7:00. At 7:15 Mary came into the restaurant, saw Tom, and walked over to say hello. Tom's dinner was still in front of him. He hadn't finished it yet. In other words, when Mary walked into the restaurant, Tom (*eat*)

_____ dinner for fifteen minutes. Tom's dinner had been in progress for fifteen minutes when Mary arrived.

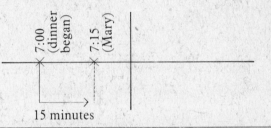

9. Tomorrow Tom will begin dinner at 7:00 and finish at 7:30. His mother will come into the kitchen at 8:00. In other words, Tom (*eat, already*)

_____

dinner by the time his mother walks into the kitchen.

12. Tonight Tom will go to a restaurant. He will begin to eat at 7:00. At 7:15 Mary will come into the restaurant, see Tom, and walk over to say hello. Tom's dinner will still be in front of him. He won't have finished it yet. In other words, when Mary walks into the restaurant tomorrow, Tom (*eat*)

_____

dinner for fifteen minutes. Tom's dinner will have been in progress for fifteen minutes by the time Mary arrives.

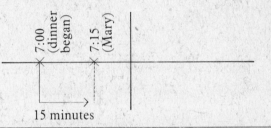

◇ PRACTICE 4—SELFSTUDY: Spelling of *-ing* and *-ed* forms. (Chart 1-6)

Part A. Directions: Write the correct *-ing* and *-ed* form for each of the following verbs.

1. shout	*shouting*	*shouted*	6. refér	....	....
2. slope	....	....	7. return	....	....
3. stop	....	....	8. enjoy	....	....
4. stoop	....	....	9. copy	....	....
5. ańswer	....	....	10. die	....	....

Part B. Directions: Write the correct *-ing* form for each of the following verbs.

11. point	*pointing*	16. regrét	....
12. beat	....	17. attempt	....
13. bet	....	18. shout	....
14. excite	....	19. flit	....
15. éxit	....	20. interest	....

Part C. Directions: Write the correct *-ed* form for each of the following verbs.

21. bóther	*bothered*	26. star	....
22. blur	....	27. stare	....
23. scare	....	28. órder	....
24. scar	....	29. súffer	....
25. fear	....	30. occúr	....

Part D. Directions: Write the correct *-ing* form for each of the following verbs.

31. dream	*dreaming*	36. deny	....
32. file	....	37. scrub	....
33. fill	....	38. drain	....
34. fail	....	39. fan	....
35. annoy	....	40. interrupt	....

Part E. Directions: Write the correct *-ed* form for each of the following verbs.

41. comb	*combed*	47. whip	....
42. wrap	....	48. accept	....
43. groan	....	49. permít	....
44. occupy	....	50. mérit	....
45. spray	....	51. whísper	....
46. wipe	....	52. infér	....

Directions: Use either the SIMPLE PRESENT or the PRESENT PROGRESSIVE of the verbs in the list to complete the sentences. Include any words given in parentheses. Use each verb only one time.

belong	fail	scream	tape
bite	fight	✔ shine	try
bleed	mean	shrink	whisper
blow	✔ own	sleep	

1. It's a gray day today. The sun (not) _____isn't shining_____.

2. The bank lent us money for a downpayment, so now we __own__ the house we used to rent.

3. Shhhh! I _____ to concentrate. I can't hear myself think with all that noise going on.

4. This book is mine. That one _____ to Pierre.

5. As a rule, I _____ until 7 o'clock in the morning, and then I get up and study for my classes.

6. A: Juan! What's the matter with your hand? It _____.

   B: I just now cut it when I was using a knife. It's not serious. I'll wash it and put a bandage on it.

7. A: My marks in school are terrible this term. I _____ three of my courses.

   B: Maybe you can improve your grades before the end of the term if you start studying harder.

8. That sweater won't fit you if you wash it in hot water. Wool _____ in hot water.

9. Look at Joan. She _____ her fingernails. She must be nervous.

10. The children can't get their kite high up in the air because the wind (not) _____ _____ hard enough today.

11. My two children don't get along. It seems they (always) _____ about something. Is that typical of siblings?

12. You can hear Tommy all over the house. Why (he) _____? I'd better see what's wrong.

13. I want to figure out the meaning of this saying: "The pen is mightier than the sword." I know that "mightier" _____ "more powerful," but what's a "sword?"

14. Alice and John! Why (you) _____ to each other? If you have something important to say, say it aloud to all of us.

15. Kareem has his tape recorder on his desk. He _____ the professor's lecture today.

◇ **PRACTICE 6—SELFSTUDY: Nonprogressive and progressive verbs. (Chart 1-9)**

Directions: Use either the SIMPLE PRESENT or the PRESENT PROGRESSIVE of the verbs in parentheses.

1. Tim (*have*) _____ **has** _____ a car.

2. Tim (*have*) _____ **is having** _____ trouble with his car, so he has to take the bus to work these days.

3. This box (*weigh*) _____ a lot. It's too heavy for me to lift.

4. I just handed the box to the postal worker. Right now she (*weigh*) _____ it to see how much postage it (*need*) _____.

5. I (*do*) _____ this practice at the moment. It (*consist*) _____ of both nonprogressive and progressive verbs.

6. I (*think*) _____ about the verbs in this grammar practice right now. I (*think*) _____ all of my answers are correct, but I'll use the answer key to check them when I finish just to make sure.

7. Mrs. Edwards is at the market. Right now she (*look*) _____ at the apples. They (*look*) _____ fresh.

8. Right now Martha is in the science building. The chemistry experiment she's doing is dangerous, so she (*be*) _____ very careful. She (*want, not*) _____ _____ to spill any of the acid. She (*be, always*) _____ careful when she does a chemistry experiment.

◇ **PRACTICE 7—GUIDED STUDY: The simple present and the present progressive.**
(Charts 1-7 → 1-10)

Directions: Use either the SIMPLE PRESENT or the PRESENT PROGRESSIVE of the verbs in parentheses.

1. Dennis (*drink, usually*) _____ **usually drinks** _____ coffee with his breakfast, but this morning he (*drink*) _____ **is drinking** _____ tea instead.

2. Janet (*take*) _____ the bus to work every day. She (*wait, usually*)

   _____ for the bus at the corner of 5th and Pine.

3. This morning it (*rain*) _____. I can see Janet from my window. She

   (*stand*) _____ at the corner of 5th and Pine. She (*hold*) _____

   her umbrella over her head. She (*wait*) _____ for the bus.

4. Mike (*take*) _____ three classes this semester. Every morning he (*study*)

   _____ for two hours before he goes to school. He (*have*) _____

   French class at 9 o'clock. He (*take, also*) _____ chemistry and

   accounting. He (*like*) _____ chemistry best of all, but he (*have*)

   _____ better grades in accounting and French.

5. MOTHER: Susie! Get your fingers out of the dessert! What (*do, you*) _____?

   SUSIE: I (*taste*) _____ the cake. It (*taste*) _____

      good.

   MOTHER: Well, you'll just have to wait until dinnertime. You can have some then.

6. JANICE: What (*write, you*) _____ in your notebook?

   DIANE: I (*make*) _____ notes about questions I want to ask the teacher.

   JANICE: (*Prepare, you, always*) _____ so thoroughly for

      every class?

   DIANE: I (*try, always*) _____ to.

7. BOB: Jack really makes me angry!

   SUE: Why?

   BOB: Well, for one thing, he (*interrupt, always*) _____ me. I

      can barely get a whole sentence out of my mouth.

   SUE: Is that all?

   BOB: No. He (*ask, always*) _____ me to do his homework for him. I have

      enough homework of my own without doing his homework too!

8. ALFONSO: What's that?

   NURSE: A needle. I (*prepare*) _____ to give you a shot.

   ALFONSO: I (*need, not*) _____ a shot!

   NURSE: Just relax and breathe deeply.

      Everything will be fine.

   ALFONSO: Ouch!

◇ PRACTICE 8—GUIDED STUDY: Irregular verbs. (Chart 1-11)

Directions: The following is a review of the forms of irregular verbs. The simple form is given. You are to provide the SIMPLE PAST and the PAST PARTICIPLE. *Note:* Verbs followed by an asterisk (*) are defined at the end of this practice (page 12).

GROUP 1: ALL THREE FORMS ARE DIFFERENT					
Group 1A: The vowel changes from "i" to "a" to "u":					
begin	*began*	*begun*	sink*	_____	_____
drink	_____	_____	spring*	_____	_____
ring	_____	_____	stink*	_____	_____
shrink*	_____	_____	swim	_____	_____
sing	_____	_____			

Group 1B: The vowel changes in the simple past. The past participle ends in "n":					
blow	*blew*	*blown*	get	_____	_____
draw	_____	_____	forget	_____	_____
grow	_____	_____			
know	_____	_____	mistake	_____	_____
throw	_____	_____	shake	_____	_____
fly	_____	_____	take	_____	_____
break	_____	_____	bite	_____	_____
choose	_____	_____	hide	_____	_____
drive	_____	_____			
freeze	_____	_____	be	_____	_____
ride	_____	_____	eat	_____	_____
rise	_____	_____	fall	_____	_____
speak	_____	_____	forgive	_____	_____
steal	_____	_____	give	_____	_____
swear	_____	_____	lie	_____	_____
tear	_____	_____	see	_____	_____
wear	_____	_____			
weave*	_____	_____	do	_____	_____
write	_____	_____	go	_____	_____

GROUP 2:   TWO FORMS ARE THE SAME: THE SIMPLE PAST AND THE PAST PARTICIPLE

Group 2A: The simple past and the past participle end in "d":

sell	*sold*	*sold*	lay		
tell			pay		
			say		
flee*					
bleed			find		
breed*			grind*		
feed			wind*		
lead					
read			have		
speed			hear		

Group 2B: The simple past and the past participle end in "t":

creep*	*crept*	*crept*	bring		
deal*			buy		
feel			catch		
keep			fight		
kneel			seek*		
leave			teach		
mean			think		
meet					
sleep			bend		
sweep			build		
weep*			lend		
			send		
lose			spend		

Group 2C: The vowel changes to form the simple past and past participle:

cling*	*clung*	*clung*	hold		
dig			shoot		
hang			sit		
spin*			stand		
stick			understand		
sting*			win		
strike*					
swing*					

Group 2D:	Only the simple past is different:		
become	*became*	*become*	
come			
run			

Group 3:	All three forms are the same					
bet*	*bet*	*bet*		put		
bid*				quit		
broadcast*				shed*		
burst*				shut		
cost				slit*		
cut				split*		
hit				spread*		
hurt				upset		
let						

*Definitions of some of the less frequently used irregular verbs:

bet ....wager; offer to pay money if one is wrong
bid ....offer as a price, usually at a public sale
breed ....bring animals together to produce young
broadcast ...send information by radio waves; announce
burst ....explode, break suddenly
cling ....hold onto tightly
creep ....crawl close to the ground; move slowly and quietly
deal ....give out playing cards to each person; give attention to (*deal with*)
flee ....escape, run away
grind ....crush, reducing to small pieces
seek ....look for
shed ....drop off or get rid of
shrink ......become smaller
sink ....drop down deeper and deeper into a liquid, usually water
slit ....cut a long, narrow opening along a line
spin ....turn rapidly around a central point
split ....divide into two or more parts
spread ......push out in all directions (e.g., butter on bread, news)
spring ......jump or rise suddenly from a still position
sting ....cause pain with a sharp object (e.g., pin) or small bite (e.g., by an insect)
stink ....have a bad or foul odor
strike ....hit something with force
swing......move back and forth
weave ......form by passing pieces of material over and under each other (e.g., baskets, cloth)
weep ....cry heavily
wind ....turn around and around

◇ PRACTICE 9—SELFSTUDY: Simple past of irregular verbs. (Chart 1-11)

Directions: Complete the sentences with the SIMPLE PAST of the irregular verbs in the list. Pay special attention to spelling. Use each verb only one time.

burst	draw	slide	stick
buy	hide	slit	✔ swear
dig	shake	spread	win

1. All of the witnesses _____**swore**_____ to tell the truth in the court of law.

2. Mike was so cold that his whole body _____.

3. Using only a pen with blue ink, Sue _____ a beautiful picture of a bird.

4. When the balloon _____, everyone was startled by the sudden noise.

5. Paul _____ his money because he was afraid it would be stolen while he was away.

6. Emily accidentally _____ her finger with a needle while she was sewing.

7. Janice _____ the top of the envelope with a knife instead of ripping it open.

8. I lost control of my car and it _____ across the ice.

9. Mary _____ butter all over her piece of toast with her knife.

10. Our team finally _____ the soccer game by one goal.

11. The small animal _____ a hole in the ground to make her nest.

12. When Fred went shopping yesterday, he _____ some car wax and a garden hose.

◇ PRACTICE 10—SELFSTUDY: Simple past of irregular verbs. (Chart 1-11)

Directions: Complete the sentences with the SIMPLE PAST of the irregular verbs in the list. Pay special attention to spelling. Use each verb only one time.

bite	cling	pay	sting
blow	feel	quit	swim
catch	mean	shed	weave

1. I broke a tooth when I _____ into a piece of hard candy.

2. The little boy _____ to his mother's hand as they walked toward the school bus.

3. Maria promised to help us. I hope she _____ what she said.

4. Arthur _____
out all of the candles on
his birthday cake.

5. We both _____ smoking three months ago, and we already feel much better.

6. Douglas _____ the outside of his pocket to make sure his wallet was still there.

7. A bee _____ me on the hand while I was working in the garden.

8. Matthew Webb was the first person who _____ across the English Channel.

9. Paul _____ much more for his bicycle than I spent for mine.

10. Rita threw the ball high in the air. Daniel _____ it when it came down.

11. Each year as the snake grew larger, it formed a new skin and _____ its old skin.

12. Everyone in Ali's family has a special skill. His sister _____ that beautiful carpet.

◇ **PRACTICE 11—SELFSTUDY: Simple past of irregular verbs. (Chart 1-11)**

Directions: Complete the sentences with the SIMPLE PAST of the irregular verbs in the list. Pay special attention to spelling. Each verb is used only one time.

bet	*freeze*	*sink*	*split*
choose	*lead*	*spend*	*upset*
fly	*ring*	*spin*	*weep*

1. Dr. Perez _____ ten hours in the operating room performing the delicate surgery.

2. On my first day at the university, Sally _____ the way to our classroom. I followed.

3. We made a friendly wager on the game. I _____ a dollar on my team.

4. I _____ when I heard the tragic news. Everyone else cried too.

5. As she stood, she _____ the table, and everything on top of it fell to the floor.

6. Paul wanted to make a fire, but the logs were too big. So he _____ them with his ax.

7. When I threw a piece of wood from the shore, it floated on top of the water. When I threw a rock, it _____ immediately to the bottom of the lake.

8. In 1927, Charles Lindbergh _____ from New York to Paris in 33 hours and 30 minutes. How long does it take today on an SST? (*SST = supersonic transport*)

9. When the children _____ around and around, they became dizzy.

10. The telephone _____ several times and then stopped before I could answer it.

11. William had trouble deciding which one he liked best, but he finally _____ the blue sweater.

12. When my cat heard a noise in the bushes, she _____ in her tracks (i.e., stopped moving completely) and listened intently.

◇ **PRACTICE 12—SELFSTUDY: Simple past of irregular verbs. (Chart 1-11)**

Directions: Complete the sentences with the SIMPLE PAST of the irregular verbs in the list. Pay special attention to spelling. Each verb is used only one time.

broadcast	fall	lose	steal
cost	flee	seek	strike
deal	hold	shoot	sweep

1. Ron had a small accident. He _____ to the floor when his foot got caught in the rug.

2. The car that Barb was driving went out of control and _____ a stop sign. That's the first time Barb ever hit anything with her car.

3. All of the radio and TV stations _____ the news of the peace plan yesterday.

4. When Mrs. Grant was having trouble, she _____ help from her neighbors. She asked them for their support and advice.

5. The team played badly. They _____ the game by seven points. Oh, well. You can't win 'em all.

6. When we played cards, Jane _____ five cards to each player.

7. Sue _____ the knife in her right hand and the fork in her left hand.

8. The hunter slowly raised his rifle and _____ at the deer, but he missed.

9. Jenny wanted a color TV for her apartment, but the least expensive one _____ too much for her budget, so she decided to wait until she could save enough money.

10. When I spilled rice on the floor, I got the broom and _____ it up.

11. A thief broke into Carlos' apartment and _____ his TV and his stereo set.

12. Tommy wanted to play a little joke on his friend, Marcia. He ran up to Marcia's front door, rang the doorbell, and then _____ quickly down the street. When Marcia answered the door, no one was there.

◇ **PRACTICE 13—GUIDED STUDY: Simple past of irregular verbs. (Chart 1-11)**

Directions: Write sentences in past time using the following verbs. Be sure to use the SIMPLE PAST.

Example:
grind → *After dinner, Maria ground some coffee beans in order to make a pot of coffee.*

1. weep	5. shake	9. creep
2. spin	6. spread	10. cling
3. seek	7. flee	11. choose
4. shed	8. split	12. sink

◇ PRACTICE 14—SELFSTUDY: Troublesome verbs, *rise/raise, sit/set, lie/lay.*
(Chart in Exercise 18)

Directions: Select the correct verb in parentheses.

1. Mr. Faust (*raises, rises*) many different kinds of flowers in his garden.

2. The student (*raised, rose*) from her seat and walked to the front of the auditorium to receive her diploma.

3. Mike (*set, sat*) a large vase with roses in it on the coffee table.

4. Claudia and Paulo (*set, sat*) next to each other at the lecture last night.

5. Hiroki is a very methodical person. Every night before going to bed, he (*lays, lies*) his clothes for the next day on his chair.

6. Wouldn't you prefer to be (*lying, laying*) on the beach right now instead of sitting in this class?

7. When Alex (*lay, laid*) down to take a nap, he ended up sleeping for the whole afternoon.

8. Where are my keys? I (*lay, laid*) them here on the desk five minutes ago.

9. Dr. Singh (*hung, hanged*) his diploma from medical school on the wall in his office.

10. Canada (*lies, lays*) to the north of the United States.

11. The fulfillment of all your dreams (*lies, lays*) within you—if you just believe in yourself.

◇ PRACTICE 15—SELFSTUDY: The simple past and the past progressive.
(Charts 1-12 → 1-14)

Directions: Fill in the blanks with the SIMPLE PAST or the PAST PROGRESSIVE of the verbs in parentheses. Include any other words in parentheses.

1. We (*have*) ____*had*____ a wonderful dinner last night to celebrate our 25th wedding anniversary.

2. We (*have, at home*) _____*were at home having*_____ our anniversary dinner when my uncle called to congratulate us last night.

3. A: Why is Henry in the hospital?

   B: He (*work, in his garage*) _____ on his car when the gas tank (*explode*) _____.

   A: What (*cause*) _____ the explosion?

   B: Henry (*light*) _____ a cigarette.

4. A: I'm sorry, Officer. I (*see, not*) _____ the stop sign. I (*think*) _____ _____ about something else.

   B: What (*think, you*) _____ about? You should have been thinking about your driving.

5. Bill asked me to come over to his apartment, but I (*want, not*) _____ to leave the house because I (*wait*) _____ for a phone call.

6. Amy (*hear, not*) _____ her parents having an argument last night. She (*listen, in her room*) _____ to music.

7. When Richard (*stop*) _____ his car suddenly, the groceries (*fall*) _____ out of the bag they were in and (*spill*) _____ all over the floor of the car.

8. When the door-to-door salesperson (*come*) _____ yesterday, Claudia (*hear, not*) _____ _____ the doorbell because she (*dry, in her room*) _____ _____ her hair with her electric hair dryer.

9. When I was a child, my mother always (*serve*) _____ cookies and milk to my friends and me when we (*go*) _____ to my house after school.

10. When we (*look*) _____ in on the baby last night, he (*sleep*) _____. I think he (*dream*) _____ about something nice because he (*smile*) _____.

◇ **PRACTICE 16—GUIDED STUDY:** **The simple past and the past progressive.**
(Charts 1-12 → 1-14)

Directions: Fill in the blanks with the SIMPLE PAST or the PAST PROGRESSIVE of the verbs in parentheses.

1. Yesterday David (*cross*) _____*was crossing*_____ a street when a truck (*turn*) _____*turned*_____ the corner very fast and almost (*hit*) _____*hit*_____ him.

2. During the study period in class yesterday, it (*be*) _____ hard for me to concentrate because the student next to me (*hum*) _____.

3. Last Monday while we (*watch, in our living room*) _____ _____ an exciting game on television, the electricity (*go*) _____ out. So we (*go*) _____ outside, (*get*) _____ into the car, (*turn*) _____ on the radio, and (*listen*) _____ to the rest of the game. The next day the car battery (*be*) _____ dead.

4. The police (*outwit*) _____ a thief yesterday. They (*surround*) _____ _____ the jewelry store while he (*stuff, still inside*) _____ _____ his pockets with diamonds.

5. Yesterday we had a houseful of children for my son's sixth birthday party. In the middle of the party, the phone (*ring*) _____, so I had to leave the children alone for a moment. When I (*come*) _____ back into the room, most of the children (*still, play*) _____ _____ together nicely. But over in the corner, Bobby (*pull*) _____ _____ Annie's hair. I quickly (*run*) _____ over and (*tell*) _____ Bobby to stop.

6. TEACHER: You're late again. You were supposed to be here ten minutes ago. Where were you?
MICHAEL: I (*look*) _____ for a place to park.
TEACHER: (*Find, you*) _____ one?
MICHAEL: Yes, but it's at a parking meter that has a 15-minute limit. So every 15 minutes I'll have to go out and put some more money in the meter.
TEACHER: Maybe you should start taking the bus to school.

MICHAEL: I (*take*) _____ the bus a couple of days ago and ended up miles from school. That's why I was absent from class.

TEACHER: Oh.

◇ PRACTICE 17—GUIDED STUDY: The simple past and the past progressive.
(Charts 1-12 → 1-14)

Directions: Complete the sentences with the SIMPLE PAST or PAST PROGRESSIVE. Use any verb that seems right to you.

1. Last Saturday while Sandy _____***was cleaning***_____ out the attic, she ___***found***___ her grandmother's wedding dress.

2. Two days ago, Peter _____ all of his money out of the bank and _____ a new car. Yesterday, while he _____ to work, he lost control of his steering and _____ another car. He wasn't hurt, but the accident completely _____ his new car.

3. Last night we suddenly _____ up from a sound sleep when we _____ a noise about 3:00 A.M. I thought it was a burglar, but it was only a cat that _____ along the window sill.

4. Two days ago I _____ my friends Ann and Andy at their apartment. They _____ the dishes when I _____. They _____ quickly, and we all _____ down and _____ about old times.

5. When I _____ to/at the airport, Lisa _____ for me in the baggage claim area. As soon as she _____ me, she _____ her arms and _____ something that I couldn't hear because the people around me _____ so much noise.

6. Mary _____ outside _____ the flowers when it _____ to rain. So, of course, she _____ off the hose and let nature take care of her garden.

◇ PRACTICE 18—SELFSTUDY: The present perfect. (Chart 1-15)

Directions: Complete the sentences with the PRESENT PERFECT of the appropriate verb from the list. Use each verb only one time. Include any words given in parentheses.

cost	*grow*	*ride*	*swim*
drive	*improve*	*save*	*win*
✔ *eat*	*know*	*start*	*write*
forget	*make*	*sweep*	

1. A: How about some more pie?

   B: No, but thanks. I can't swallow another bite. I (*already*) _____***have already eaten***_____ too much.

2. Our football team is having a great season. They _____ all but one of their games so far this year and will probably win the championship.

3. Jane is expecting a letter from me, but I (*not*) _____ to her yet. Maybe I'll call her instead.

4. Jack is living in Spain now. His Spanish used to be terrible, but it _____ greatly since he moved there.

5. Our baby (*not*) _____ to talk yet. My friend's baby, who is several months older, can already say a few words in English and a few words in French.

6. A: I hear your parents are coming to visit you. Is that why you're cleaning your apartment?

   B: You guessed it! I (*already*) _____ the floor, but I still need to dust the furniture. Want to help?

7. A: I understand Tom is a good friend of yours? How long (*you*) _____ him?

   B: Since we were kids.

8. Everyone makes mistakes in life. I _____ lots of mistakes in my life. The important thing is to learn from one's mistakes. Right?

9. A: I (*never*) _____ on the subway in New York City. Have you?

   B: I've never even been in New York City.

10. A: (*You, ever*) _____ in the Atlantic Ocean?

    B: No, only the Pacific—when I was in Hawaii. I even went snorkeling when I was there.

11. Little Freddie _____ a lot since I last saw him. He's going to be tall just like his father, isn't he?

12. Let's stop at the next motel. We _____ 500 miles so far today and that's enough.

13. Simon spoke Arabic when he lived in Lebanon as a young child, but now he _____ _____ almost all of his Arabic. He remembers only a few words.

14. Maintaining this old car for the past five years _____ us much less than we would have spent if we had bought a new one. We _____ a lot of money by not buying a new car, haven't we?

◇ **PRACTICE 19—SELFSTUDY: Using *since* and *for*. (Chart 1-15)**

Directions: Write either *since* or *for* in the blanks.

1. I haven't seen my brother ____*for*____ 6 months. I haven't seen my sister ____*since*____ April.

2. My wife and I have moved three times _____ we got married.

3. We've lived here _____ three years, but we're going to move again soon.

4. The Smiths have lived here _____ a long time. They've lived here _____ 1970.

5. My sister's husband got a job on a fishing boat in Alaska. He's been there _____ eleven weeks, but he should be coming home soon.

6. The International Olympic Games have continued almost without interruption _____ 1896.

7. The world has enjoyed Beethoven's music _____ nearly 200 years.

8. They have been married _____ last summer.

9. The first sections of the Great Wall of China have endured _____ a long time. They have endured _____ more than 2,200 years.

10. Overall, Ed hasn't learned very much _____ the term began. He needs to study harder.

11. The clock on the campus tower hasn't moved _____ 3:13 on March 2, 1966. Nobody has been able to fix the clock _____ that time.

12. Argentina won The World Cup in 1986 for the second time _____ the cup was first awarded in 1930. Soccer is a popular sport there.

◇ **PRACTICE 20—SELFSTUDY: The simple past and the present perfect. (Charts 1-12 and 1-15)**

Directions: Complete the sentences with the SIMPLE PAST or PRESENT PERFECT of the verb in parentheses.

1. I ___*knew*___ Tim when he was a child, but I haven't seen him for many years. I ___*have*___ ___*known*___ Larry, my best friend, for more than 20 years. (*know*)

2. The company and the union finally ___*agreed*___ on salary raises two days ago. Since then, they ___*have agreed*___ on everything, and the rest of the negotiations have gone smoothly. (*agree*)

3. Mark ___*took*___ a trip to Asia last October. He ___*has taken*___ many trips to Asia since he started his own import–export business. (*take*)

4. Ivan ___*has played*___ the violin with the London Symphony since 1985. Last year he ___*played*___ a Beethoven violin concerto at one of the concerts. (*play*)

5. When she was in college, Julia ___*wrote*___ home at least once each week. Now she has a job and is living in Chicago. In the last six months, she ___*has written*___ only three letters to her parents. (*write*)

6. Our university ___*sent*___ 121 students to study in other countries last year. In total, we ___*have sent*___ 864 students abroad over the last ten years. (*send*)

7. Masaru is a pilot for JAL. He _____ nearly 8 million miles during the last 22 years. Last year, he _____ 380,000 miles. (*fly*)

8. Mark missed his physics examination this morning because he _____. He _____ a lot since the beginning of the semester. He'd better buy a new alarm clock. (*oversleep*)

9. Alex is an artist. He _____ many beautiful pictures in his lifetime. Last week, he _____ a beautiful mountain scene. (*draw*)

10. Jack really needs to get in touch with you. Since this morning, he _____ here four times trying to reach you. He _____ at 9:10, 10:25, 12:15, and 1:45. (*call*)

11. Janet _____ her new blue dress only once since she bought it. She _____ it to her brother's wedding. (*wear*)

12. The night has ended and it's daylight now. The sun _____. It _____ at 6:08. (*rise*)

◇ PRACTICE 21—GUIDED STUDY: The present perfect. (Chart 1-15)

Directions: Write answers to the following questions.

1. What significant changes have taken place in your life since you were thirteen years old?
2. What are some interesting experiences you have had in your lifetime?
3. What are some things you have not yet done in your lifetime but would like to do?
4. Who are some of the people you've met and what are some of the things you have done since the beginning of the term?
5. Where are some of the places you've visited in the world or in your country, and when did you visit them?

◇ PRACTICE 22—SELFSTUDY: The present perfect and the present perfect progressive.
                            (Charts 1-15 and 1-16)

Directions: Use either the PRESENT PERFECT or the PRESENT PERFECT PROGRESSIVE of the given verbs.

1. The children are at the park. They (*play*) __*have been playing*__ ball for the last two hours, but they don't seem to be tired yet.

2. Jim (*play*) __*has played*__ soccer only a couple of times, so he's not very good at it. He's much better at tennis.

3. A: Janice (*sleep*) _____ for almost eleven hours. Don't you think we should wake her up?

   B: I guess we probably should.

4. Tim (*sleep*) _____ in the downstairs bedroom only once. He usually sleeps upstairs in the bedroom he shares with his brother.

5. I (*fly, not*) _____ on a plane since last year when I was on a plane that had a fire in one of its engines. Now I'm afraid to even think about getting on an airplane.

6. A: How much longer until we arrive at the Singapore airport?

   B: Let me see. It's about 9:15. We (*fly*) _____ for almost six hours. We should be there in another couple of hours.

7. A: Is the rescue crew still looking for survivors of the plane crash?

   B: Yes, they (*search*) _____ the area for hours, but

   they haven't found anybody else. They'll keep searching until night falls.

8. Karl (*raise*) _____ three children to adulthood. Now they are educated and

   working in productive careers.

9. Sally is falling asleep at her desk. Dr. Wu (*lecture*) _____

   since ten and it's now past noon.

10. Virginia is a law student. Ever since she enrolled in law school, she (*miss, never*) _____

    _____ a day of class due to illness.

11. The club members (*make, finally*) _____ their decision. The

    election is over, and they (*choose*) _____ a new president. Ann Andrews

    is now the club leader.

12. Since I bought my son a set of drums, the noise (*drive*) _____

    my wife and me crazy, but I suppose we'll get used to it pretty soon.

◇ **PRACTICE 23—GUIDED STUDY: The present perfect and the present perfect progressive.
                                (Charts 1-15 and 1-16)**

Directions: Complete the sentences by using the PRESENT PERFECT or PRESENT PERFECT
PROGRESSIVE of the words in the list. Include any words in parentheses. Each verb is used only
one time.

cook	hear	spend	✔ understand
dig	meet	stand	wait
grow	paint	travel	want

1. They have never gotten along with each other. I (*never*) _____*have never understood*_____ why they agreed to be roommates in the first place.

2. Al just introduced me to his sister. Now I _____ everyone in his family.

3. Ms. Erickson is a sales clerk in a large department store. It's almost closing time. Her feet hurt, as they do every day, because she _____ at the sales counter since eight o'clock this morning.

4. A: I am so happy! I finally got the one thing that I (*always*) _____
   B: What's that?

5. My uncle _____ the outside of his house for three weeks and he's still not finished. He's being very careful. He wants his house to look just right.

6. The Smiths are presently in Tunisia. They _____ throughout North Africa since the middle of May. They'll return home in another month.

7. My brother's daughter _____ nearly six inches (15 cm) since I last saw her two years ago.

8. A: How much money do you have to buy clothes with?
   B: Sixty dollars.
   A: I thought you had a hundred dollars.
   B: I did. But I (*already*) _____ forty.

9. A: Isn't the rice ready to eat yet? It _____ for over an hour, hasn't it? Are you sure you know how to cook rice?
   B: Of course I do! I've watched my mother make rice for years.

10. I'm surprised that George apologized for what he said. As far as I can remember, I (*never*) _____ him say "I'm sorry" before.

11. A: We _____ to hear about the new baby since 5 A.M. Isn't there any word yet?
    B: Not yet.

12. A: I've been watching Mr. Tuttle in his front yard across the street. He _____ a long trench across the middle of his yard for the last two hours. I wonder why.
    B: He's uncovering the water pipes so he can repair a leak and put in new plumbing.

◇ **PRACTICE 24—GUIDED STUDY:** Writing.

Directions: Describe your first day in this class. What did you see, hear, feel, think? Then write about what you have done and have been doing in this class since the first day.

◇ PRACTICE 25—SELFSTUDY: The simple past and the past perfect. (Charts 1-12 and 1-17)

Directions: Use the PAST PERFECT or the SIMPLE PAST of the verbs in the list to complete the sentences. Include any words in parentheses. Use each verb only once.

be	✔ finish	invent	sting
burn	fly	leave	teach
design	help	spend	✔ turn on

1. By the time Jason arrived to help, we (*already*) _____**had already finished**_____ moving everything.

2. The apartment was hot when I got home, so I _____**turned on**_____ the air conditioner.

3. Alexander Graham Bell (*already*) _____ the telephone by the time I was born.

4. The farmer's barn caught fire some time during the night. By the time the firefighters arrived, the building _____ to the ground. It was a total loss.

5. The suit I bought cost more than a week's salary. Until then, I (*never*) _____ _____ so much on one outfit.

6. Yesterday a hornet _____ me under my arm. That really hurt! When I put on my shirt after working in the garden, I hadn't seen that there was a hornet in it.

7. We were not happy with the plans that the architect showed us for our new house. Obviously, he (*never*) _____ a home like the one we wanted.

8. When I saw that Mike was having trouble, I _____ him. He was very appreciative.

9. My wife and I went to Disneyland when we visited Los Angeles last spring. Prior to that time, we (*never*) _____ to such a big amusement park. It was a lot of fun.

10. Last year I experienced how tedious long plane trips can be. I _____ in an airplane for fairly long distances before, but never as long as when I went to Australia last June.

11. Mr. Khan has had experience teaching chemistry and physics, but he (*not*) _____ _____ mathematics until this year. He's found that he enjoys teaching math.

12. Promptly at five, I went to Iris' office to offer her a ride home from work, but when I got to her office, I couldn't find her. She (*already*) _____.

◇ PRACTICE 26—SELFSTUDY: The simple past and the past perfect. (Charts 1-12 and 1-17)

Directions: Use the SIMPLE PAST or the PAST PERFECT of the verbs in parentheses. In some cases, both forms are correct.

1. Yesterday I (*go*) _____**went**_____ to my daughter's dance recital. I (*be, never*) _____**had never been**_____ to a dance recital before. I (*take, not*) _____**didn't take**_____ dancing lessons when I (*be*) _____**was**_____ a child.

2. Last night, I (*eat*) _____ four servings of food at the "all-you-can-eat" special dinner at The Village Restaurant. Until that time, I (*eat, never*) _____ so much in one meal. I've felt miserable all day today.

3. A friend of mine, Judith Nelson, is presently working in the international sales division at an electronics firm. She's just returned from a trip to Japan. She was asked to go to Japan because she can speak Japanese. When she (*be*) _____ a business student at Boston University, she (*study*) _____ Japanese for four years. She (*have, never*) _____ the opportunity to use her Japanese until she went to Tokyo last month. While she was there, she (*speak*) _____ Japanese every day and (*enjoy*) _____ every minute of it. She's anxious to return.

4. A: I (*see*) _____ you in the school play last night. You (*do*) _____ a terrific acting job. (*Act, you, ever*) _____ in a play before this one?

   B: Yes. I (*start*) _____ acting when I was in elementary school.

5. Last year, I (*go*) _____ mountain climbing for the first time. It was exciting and terrifying at the same time. We (*move*) _____ slowly and carefully, and it (*take*) _____ three days to get to the top. Imagine our surprise when we climbed onto the summit and found another group of climbers. They (*arrive*) _____ several hours ahead of us. They were having dinner and listening to Beethoven. We (*laugh*) _____, and they (*invite*) _____ us to join them. The climb (*be*) _____, to say the least, an unforgettable experience.

6. When I first (*travel*) _____ abroad to study, I (*live, never*) _____ in a dormitory before. During the first year, I (*have*) _____ a roommate from Switzerland who (*become*) _____ a very good friend. Prior to that time, I (*live, never*) _____ with anyone from another culture.

7. In 1955, my parents (*emigrate*) _____ to the United States from Turkey. They (*travel, never*) _____ outside of Turkey and were, of course, excited by the challenge of relocating in a foreign country. Eventually, they (*settle*) _____ in California. My sister and I were born there and (*grow*) _____ up there. Last year, I (*go*) _____ to Turkey for the first time to visit my relatives. I (*want, always*) _____ to visit Turkey and learn more about my own family background. My dream was finally realized.

◇ **PRACTICE 27—GUIDED STUDY: The past perfect. (Chart 1-17)**

Directions: Complete the following sentences with your own words.

1. I had never...before I....
2. By the time..., he had already....
3. In 1987, I....   Prior to that time, I had....
4. When I..., someone else had already....
5. Last January, I....   Before that, I had never....
6. I had never...until I....
7. The movie had...by the time we....
8. My...after I had already....

◇ **PRACTICE 28—SELFSTUDY: The present perfect progressive and the past perfect progressive. (Charts 1-16 and 1-18)**

Directions: Use the PRESENT PERFECT PROGRESSIVE or the PAST PERFECT PROGRESSIVE to complete the following sentences.

1. Anna (*listen to*) _____*had been listening to*_____ loud rock music when her friends arrived but turned it off so all of them could study together. When they finished, she turned it back on, and they (*dance*) _____*have been dancing*_____ and (*sing*) _____*singing*_____ for two hours now.

2. We (*wait*) _____ for Nancy for the last two hours, but she still hasn't arrived.

3. We (*wait*) _____ for Nancy for over three hours before she finally arrived yesterday.

4. Oscar (*train*) _____ for the Olympics for the last three years and wants to make the national team next year.

5. The marathon runner (*run*) _____ for almost two hours when she collapsed to the pavement. She received immediate medical attention.

6. Tom had a hard time finding a job. He (*try*) _____ to get a new job for six months before he finally found a position at a local community college. Now he has a two-year contract. He (*teach*) _____ there for only a few weeks, but he likes his new job very much.

7. Dr. Sato (*perform*) _____ specialized surgery since she began working at the university hospital ten years ago. She still does many operations each year, but now her work is so famous that she travels all over the world lecturing to other surgeons on her technique.

8. The Acme Construction Company is having problems. They (*work*) _____ _____ on a new office building for the last seven months, and everything seems to be going wrong. Earlier, they stopped work on a smaller structure that they (*build*) _____ _____ so they could take on this job. Now both projects are in jeopardy.

◇ PRACTICE 29—GUIDED STUDY: Writing.

Directions: Choose one of the following topics and write a composition.

1. Write a brief history of your country.
2. Write a brief history of your family.
3. Write a brief history of your education since early childhood.

◇ PRACTICE 30—SELFSTUDY: *Will* vs. *be going to*. (Charts 1-19 and 1-20)

Directions: Complete the sentences with *will* or *be going to*, as appropriate. Include any words in parentheses.

1. A: Excuse me, waiter! This isn't what I ordered. I ordered a chicken sandwich.

   B: Sorry, sir. I _____*will*_____ take this back and get your sandwich.

   A: Thank you.

2. A: Would you like to join Linda and me tomorrow? We _____*are going to*_____ visit the natural history museum.

   B: Sure. I've never been there.

3. A: Where's the mustard?

   B: In the refrigerator, on the middle shelf.

   A: I've looked there.

   B: Okay. I _____ find it for you.

4. A: What's all this paint for? (*You*) _____ paint your house?

   B: No, we _____ paint my mother's house.

5. A: Paul, do you want to go with me to the shopping mall?

   B: No thanks. I have some things I have to do today. I _____ wash my car and then clean out the basement.

6. A: Someone needs to take this report to Mr. Day's office right away, but I can't leave my desk.

   B: I _____ do it.

   A: Thanks.

7. A: Let's make something easy for dinner. Got any ideas?

   B: I _____ make some hamburgers. Why don't you make a salad?

   A: Sounds good.

8. A: Why did you buy so many tomatoes?

   B: I _____ make a lot of spaghetti sauce.

◇ **PRACTICE 31—GUIDED STUDY:** *Will* vs. *be going to.* (Charts 1-19 and 1-20)

Directions: Complete the sentences with *will* or the correct form of *be going to*, as appropriate. Include any words in parentheses.

1. A: Who'd like to take the VCR back to the visual aids room? Any volunteers?

   B: I _____ do it.

2. A: Why did you buy so many vegetables?

   B: I _____ make a large salad for the potluck dinner tonight.

3. A: Why is Carlos wearing a suit and tie? He usually wears jeans to class.

   B: He _____ give a speech at the faculty lunch today.

   A: Really? What (*he*) _____ speak about?

   B: About university study in his country.

4. A: I wonder what the weather is like in Chicago now. I need to know what kind of clothes to pack for my trip there.

   B: I don't know, but it just so happens that I have a cousin who lives in Chicago, and I have to call her tonight. I _____ ask her about the weather and tell you what she says.

5. A: Jack, I need a favor.

   B: What can I do, Andy?

   A: I _____ go to a job interview this afternoon, and I don't have a decent tie to wear.

   B: I _____ lend you one of mine.

   A: Thanks.

6. A: Are you going out?

   B: I _____ go to the grocery store for some fruit, meat, and rice. Can you think of anything else we need?

   A: How about some chocolate-covered nuts?

   B: I said ''need''!

7. A: Janice, do you want to come with us?

   B: I can't. I have to study.

   A: Oh, c'mon! You can't study all day and all night.

   B: All right, I _____ go with you. I guess I can finish this stuff tomorrow.

8. A: How do you spell "accustomed"?

   B: I'm not sure. I _____ look it up for you.

   A: Thanks.

   B: Here it is. It has two "c's" but only one "m".

◇ PRACTICE 32—SELFSTUDY: Expressing the future in time clauses. (Charts 1-19 → 1-21)

Directions: Find the time clause in each sentence. Put brackets ([....]) around it. Notice the use of tenses.

1. We'll be here [when you arrive tomorrow.]

2. After the rain stops, I'm going to sweep the front porch.

3. I'm going to start making dinner before my wife gets home from work today.

4. As soon as the war is over, there will be great joy throughout the land.

5. I'm going to wait right here until Jessica comes.

6. Right now the tide is low, but when the tide comes in, the ship will leave the harbor.

◇ PRACTICE 33—SELFSTUDY: Expressing the future in time clauses. (Charts 1-19 → 1-21)

Directions: Complete the sentences with the SIMPLE PRESENT or with *will* and/or the correct form of *be going to*. (In some blanks, both *will* and *be going to* may be possible.)

1. The strike has been going on for over two months now. The strikers (*return, not*)
   _____**will not/are not going to return**_____ to work until they (*get*) _____**get**_____ a raise
   and the benefits they are demanding.

2. When Rita (*get*) _____ her driver's license next week, she (*be*)
   _____ able to drive to school every day.

3. A: I see you're reading *The Silk Road*. I'd really like to read it sometime.

   B: I (*lend*) _____ it to you as soon as I (*finish*) _____ it.

   A: Really? Thanks!

4. A: Have you heard any news about Barbara since her car accident?

   B: No, I've heard nothing. As soon as I (*hear*) _____ something, I (*let*)
   _____ you know.

5. A: Mr. Jackson called. He'll be here at the garage to pick up his car in a few minutes. He (*be, not*) _____ very happy when he (*learn*) _____
   about the bill for repairs on his car. Do you want to talk to him when he (*come*)
   _____ in and (*ask*) _____ about his bill?

   B: Not especially, but I will.

6. After Ali (*return*) _____ to his country next month, he (*start*)
   _____ working at the Ministry of Agriculture.

7. According to the newspaper, the Department of Transportation (*build*) _____

a four-lane highway between here and San Francisco. In my opinion, it (*be*)

_____ obsolete before they (*complete*) _____

it. It seems to me that a six-lane highway is needed to handle the heavy traffic.

8. Relax. The plumber is on his way. He (*be*) _____ here before there (*be*)

_____ a flood in the kitchen. Let's just keep mopping up the water the best

we can.

◇ **PRACTICE 34—GUIDED STUDY:** Expressing the future in time clauses. (Charts 1-19 → 1-21)

Directions: Complete the sentences with your own words.

1. After I . . . tomorrow, I . . . .
2. I'm not going to . . . until you . . . .
3. Everything will . . . as soon as . . . .
4. When . . . next week, you . . . .
5. My friend is not going to . . . until . . . .
6. When I . . . next month, the weather . . . .
7. The committee chair will . . . as soon as . . . .
8. As soon as . . . , everyone will . . . .
9. Before I . . . , I will have to . . . .
10. Please . . . before I . . . .
11. I will . . . as soon as Mr. . . . .
12. When . . . tomorrow, ...

◇ **PRACTICE 35—SELFSTUDY:** Using the present progressive to express the future. (Chart 1-22)

Directions: Use the PRESENT PROGRESSIVE form of the verbs in the list to complete the sentences.

come	✔ meet	quit
drive	pick up	see
have	play	take

1. A: How about going across the street for a cup of coffee?

B: I can't. I _____ *am meeting* _____ Jennifer at the library at 5:00.

2. A: Why are you in such a hurry?

   B: I have to be at the airport in an hour. I _____ the 4 o'clock plane to New York. I have an important meeting there tomorrow.

3. A: We got an invitation in the mail from Ron and Maureen. They _____ a dinner party next Saturday evening. Do you want to go? I'd like to.

   B: Sure. I always enjoy spending time with them. Let's call and tell them we _____

   _____.

4. A: Your cough sounds terrible! You should see a doctor.

   B: I know. It just won't go away. I _____ Dr. Murray later this afternoon.

5. A: Have you seen Jackie?

   B: She just left. She's going to the mall, and then she _____ her sister at the airport. She should be back around 4:30.

6. A: Where are you and your family going for your vacation this summer?

   B: Ontario.

   A: Are you planning to fly?

   B: No, we _____ there so we can take our time and enjoy the scenery.

7. A: We're going to a soccer match next week.

   B: Who _____?

   A: A team from Brazil against a team from Argentina. It ought to be a really exciting game.

8. A: I see you're smoking. I thought you stopped last month.

   B: I did. I don't know why I started again. I _____ again tomorrow, and this time I mean it.

◇ **PRACTICE 36—GUIDED STUDY:** Using the present progressive to express future time.
(Chart 1-22)

Directions: Change the verbs in italics to the PRESENT PROGRESSIVE for those sentences that express a planned event or definite intention. In some sentences, no change is possible.

1. A: The package has to be there tomorrow. Will it get there in time?
   B: Don't worry. I'*m going to send* it by express mail.
   → *Also possible: I'm sending it by express mail.*

2. A: What's the weather report?
   B: It *is going to rain* tomorrow morning.
   → *(Not possible: It's raining tomorrow morning.)*

3. A: Would you like to have dinner with me tonight, Pat?
   B: Thanks, but I'*m going to have* dinner with my sister and her husband.

4. A: What *are you going to do* this evening?
   B: I'*m going to study* at the library.

5. A: The phone is ringing.
   B: I'll get it.

6. A: Did you know that Bill and Sue are engaged?
   B: No. That's great! When *are they going to get* married?
   A: In September.

7. A: You're *going to laugh* when I tell you what happened to me today!
   B: Oh? What happened?

8. A: Have you lived here long?
   B: No, not long. Only about a year. But we're *going to move* again next month. My father's company has reassigned him to Atlanta, Georgia.

9. A: I tried to register for Professor Stein's economics class, but it's full. *Is he going to teach* it again next semester?
   B: I think so.

10. A: Son, I'm *not going to send* you any more money this month. You're spending far too much. You need to learn to be more careful.
    B: But Dad...!
    A: Just do the best you can. Your mother and I *are going to come* to visit you next month. We can talk about it then.

◇ **PRACTICE 37—SELFSTUDY:** The future progressive. (Charts 1-21 and 1-23)

Directions: Complete the sentences with the FUTURE PROGRESSIVE or the SIMPLE PRESENT of the verbs in parentheses.

1. Just relax, Antoine. As soon as your sprained ankle (*heal*) ___**heals**___, you can play soccer again. At this time next week, you (*play*) ___**will be playing**___ soccer again.

2. I'll meet you at the airport tomorrow. After you (*clear*) _____ customs, look for me just outside the gate. I (*stand*) _____ right by the door.

3. Ingrid and Ruth won't be at this school when classes (*start*) _____ next semester. They (*attend*) _____ a new school in Taiwan.

4. Please come and visit today when you (*have*) _____ a chance. I (*shop*) _____ from 1:00 to 2:30, but I'll be home after that.

5. I won't be here next week. I (*attend*) _____ a seminar in Chicago. Ms. Gomez will substitute teach for me. When I (*return*) _____, I will expect you to be ready for the midterm examination.

6. A: Do you think life will be very different 100 years from now?
   B: Of course. I can picture it in my mind. People (*live*) _____ in modular mobile residential units that they can take with them if they have to move, and they (*drive*) _____ air cars that can go at tremendous speeds.
   A: That sounds pretty farfetched to me. Why would people want to take their houses with them when they move?

◇ **PRACTICE 38—SELFSTUDY:** The future perfect and the future perfect progressive. (Charts 1-24 and 1-25)

Directions: Complete the sentences with the FUTURE PERFECT or the FUTURE PERFECT PROGRESSIVE of the verbs in the list. Include any words in parentheses. Use each verb only once.

arrive	listen	✔ rise	smoke
fly	ride	save	teach

1. By the time I get up tomorrow morning, the sun (*already*) ___*will already have risen/*___
   ___*will have already risen*___.

2. This is a long trip! By the time we get to Miami, we _____
   on this bus for over 15 hours.

3. We're going to be late meeting my brother's plane. By the time we get to the airport, it
   (*already*) _____.

4. He's never going to stop talking. In 15 more minutes, we _____
   _____ to him lecture for three solid hours. I don't even know what he's saying
   anymore.

5. What? You're smoking another cigarette? At this rate, you _____
   a whole pack before lunchtime. Don't you think you should cut down a little?

6. This is the longest flight I have ever taken. By the time we get to New Zealand, we
   _____ for 13 hours. I'm going to be exhausted.

7. Douglas has been putting some money away every month to prepare for his trip to South
   America next year. By the end of this year, he _____ enough. It
   looks like he's going to make it.

8. Can you believe it? According to our grammar teacher, by the end of this semester she
   _____ more than 3,000 students from 42 different countries.
   She has been teaching for nearly 20 years—and she still loves it!

◇ **PRACTICE 39—GUIDED STUDY:** Past and future. (Charts 1-12 → 1-25)

Directions: The following sentences are descriptions of typical events in a day in the life of a person named Dick. The sentences are in the past, but all of these things will happen in Dick's life tomorrow. Change all of the sentences to the FUTURE.

1. When Dick got up yesterday morning, the sun was shining.

   → *When Dick gets up tomorrow morning, the sun will be shining.*

2. He shaved and showered and then made a light breakfast.

3. After he ate breakfast, he got ready to go to work.

4. By the time he got to work, he had drunk three cups of coffee.

5. Between 8:00 and 9:00, he dictated letters and planned his day.

6. By 10:00, he had finished his account books.

7. At 11:00, he was attending a staff meeting.

8. He went to lunch at noon and had a sandwich and a bowl of soup.

9. After he finished eating, he took a short walk in the park before he returned to the office.

10. He worked at his desk until he went to another meeting in the middle of the afternoon.

11. By the time he left the office, he had attended three meetings.

12. When he got home, the children were playing in the yard.

13. They had been playing since 3:00 in the afternoon.

14. As soon as he finished dinner, he took the children for a walk to a nearby playground.

15. Afterwards, the whole family sat in the living room and discussed their day.

16. They watched television for a while, and then he and his wife put the kids to bed.

17. By the time he went to bed, Dick had had a full day and was ready for sleep.

◇ PRACTICE 40—SELFSTUDY: Review of tenses. (Chapter 1)

Directions: Complete the sentences with the verbs in parentheses. Use any appropriate tense.

On June 20th, I returned home. I (*1. be*) _____ away from home for two years. My family (*2. meet*) _____ me at the airport with kisses and tears. They (*3. miss*) _____ me as much as I had missed them. I (*4. be*) _____ very happy to see them again. When I (*5. get*) _____ the chance, I (*6. take*) _____ a long look at them. My little brother (*7. be*) _____ no longer little. He (*8. grow*) _____ at least a foot. He (*9. be*) _____ almost as tall as my father. My little sister (*10. wear*) _____ a green dress. She (*11. change*) _____ quite a bit, too, but she (*12. be, still*) _____ mischievous and inquisitive. She (*13. ask*) _____ me a thousand questions a minute, or so it seemed. My father (*14. gain*) _____ some weight, and his hair (*15. turn*) _____ a little bit grayer, but otherwise he was just as I had remembered him. My mother (*16. look*) _____ a little older, but not much. The wrinkles on her face (*17. be*) _____ smile wrinkles.

◇ PRACTICE 41—SELFSTUDY: Review of tenses. (Chapter 1)

Directions: Complete the sentences with the verbs in parentheses. Use any appropriate tense.

On June 20th, I will return home. I (*1. be*) _____ away from home for two years by that time. My family (*2. meet*) _____ me at the airport with kisses and tears. They (*3. miss*) _____ me as much as I have missed them. I (*4. be*) _____ very happy to see them again. When I (*5. get*) _____ a chance, I (*6. take*) _____ a long look at them. My little brother (*7. be, no longer*)

_____ so little. He (*8. grow*) _____

at least a foot. He (*9. be*) _____ almost as tall as my father. My little sister (*10. wear,*

probably) _____ a green dress because that's her

favorite color. She (*11. change*) _____ quite a bit, too, but she

(*12. be, still*) _____ mischievous and inquisitive. She (*13. ask*) _____

me a thousand questions a minute, or so it will seem. My father (*14. gain, probably*)

_____ some weight, and his hair (*15. turn*)

_____ a little grayer, but otherwise he will be just as I remember

him. My mother (*16. look*) _____ a little older, but not much. The wrinkles on her

face (*17. be*) _____ smile wrinkles.

◇ PRACTICE 42—GUIDED STUDY: Review of tenses. (Chapter 1)

Directions: Complete the sentences with the verbs in parentheses. Use any appropriate tense.

   I. A: Alex, (*1. you, know*) __**do you know**__ where Ms. Rodriguez is? I (*2. look*)

   _____ for her for the past hour.

   B: She (*3. see*) _____ Mr. Frost at the moment about the shipment of parts

   which we (*4. receive*) _____ earlier today. Some of the parts are missing.

   A: Oh, oh. That (*5. sound*) _____ like trouble. Please tell Ms. Rodriguez to phone

   me when she (*6. have*) _____ some free time. I (*7. work*) _____

   in my office all afternoon.

   II. A: What (*1. seem*) _____ to be the trouble, Ms. Jones?

   B: I (*2. send*) _____ in my money for a subscription to your magazine, *Computer Data,*

   two months ago, but to date I (*3. receive, not*) _____ any

   issues.

   A: I'm terribly sorry to hear that. Unfortunately, one of our main computers (*4. function, not*)

   _____ at the moment. However, our engineers

   (*5. work*) _____ very hard to fix it at the present time. We (*6. start*)

   _____ your new subscription as soon as possible.

   B: Thank you.

   III. A: Where's Sonia? I (*1. see, not*) _____ her lately.

   B: She (*2. recuperate, at home*) _____.

   A: Oh? What's she recuperating from?

   B: She (*3. hurt*) _____ her back while she (*4. play*) _____

   volleyball last week in the game against South City College.

   A: What happened? How (*5. she, hurt*) _____ her back?

B: She (6. *try*) _____ to spike a ball when she (7. *collide*)

_____ with another player and (8. *fall*) _____ to the floor. She

(9. *land*) _____ hard and (10. *twist*) _____ her back.

A: Gosh, that's too bad. I'm sorry to hear that. How's she doing?

B: Well, she's pretty uncomfortable. She (11. *wear*) _____ a

special brace on her back for the last five days. Needless to say, she (12. *be, not*)

_____ able to play volleyball since her injury. She probably (13. *be,*

not) _____ able to play again for at least a month.

A: (14. *allow, her doctor*) _____ her to play in the

national tournament at the end of the summer?

B: She (15. *have*) _____ the brace on her back for more than seven

weeks by then, so I think he will.

A: I hope so. I know how much she likes to compete in volleyball games. And the team really

needs her.

IV. A: Hi, Jim. How's it going?

B: Great.

A: (*1. You, enjoy*) _____ the rock concert last night?

B: You bet. I had a terrific time.

A: Tell me about it. I (*2. go, never*) _____ to a rock concert.

B: Well, I (*3. go, never*) _____ to a rock concert before either, so I (*4. know, not*) _____ what to expect. I've been to symphony concerts lots of times, but never a rock concert. Ten minutes before the concert was supposed to start, hundreds of teenagers (*5. try, still*) _____ to find their seats. The place was a madhouse. I thought that things would settle down once the concert began. Boy, was I wrong! As soon as the lead singer (*6. appear*) _____ on the stage, everyone (*7. start*) _____ screaming at the top of their lungs. I couldn't hear myself think. But after a while things calmed down. And the music was great. At one time during the concert, while the lead singer (*8. sing*) _____ a famous hit song, many people in the audience knew the song so well that they sang along with him. All in all, the concert (*9. be*) _____ a lot of fun, but very noisy.

A: It does sound like it was a lot of fun!

V. Mark Twain, the author of *The Adventures of Tom Sawyer*, is one of America's best-loved storytellers. He (*1. grow up*) _____ in a small town on the Mississippi River. As a young boy, he (*2. admire, greatly*) _____ the pilots of the riverboats and dreamed about being a riverboat pilot on the mighty river. He pursued his dream, and by the age of 22, he himself (*3. become*) _____ a riverboat pilot. Later in life, when he (*4. become*) _____ a writer, many of his stories (*5. contain*) _____ elements of his own experiences. He wrote many humorous stories and articles about life on the Mississippi River before he (*6. die*) _____ in 1910 at the age of 74. Sadly, Twain (*7. work*) _____ on a new story for several months before his death, but he (*8. finish, never*) _____ it. Over the years since his death, his boyhood home in Hannibal, Missouri, (*9. become* _____ a favorite place for Americans to visit to learn about Twain and life on the Mississippi at the turn of the century.

◇ **PRACTICE 43—GUIDED STUDY: Review of tenses. (Chapter 1)**

Directions: Complete the sentences with the words in parentheses. Use any appropriate tense.

Almost every part of the world (*1. experience*) _____ an earthquake in recent years, and almost every part of the world (*2. experience*) _____ earthquakes in the years to come. Since the ancient Chinese (*3. begin*) _____ to keep records thousands of years ago, more than 13 million earthquakes (*4. occur*) _____ worldwide by some estimates.

What (*5. cause*) _____ earthquakes? Throughout time, different cultures (*6. develop*) _____ myths to explain these violent earth movements.

According to a Japanese myth, a playful catfish lives in the mud under the earth. Whenever it feels like playing, it (*7. wave*) _____ its fat tail around in the mud. The result? Earthquakes. From India comes the story of six strong elephants who (*8. hold*) _____ up the earth on their heads. Whenever one elephant (*9. move*) _____ its head, the earth trembles.

Nowadays, although scientists (*10. know*) _____ more about the causes of earthquakes, they still can't prevent the terrible damage.

One of the strongest quakes in this century (*11. happen*) _____ in Anchorage, Alaska, on March 24, 1964, at about six o'clock in the evening. When the earthquake (*12. strike*) _____ that evening, many families (*13. sit*) _____ down to eat dinner. People in the city (*14. find, suddenly*) _____ themselves in the dark because most of the lights in the city went out when the earthquake occurred. Many people (*15. die*) _____ instantly when tall buildings (*16. collapse*) _____ and (*17. send*) _____ tons of brick and concrete crashing into the streets.

When (*18. occur, the next earthquake*) _____? No one really knows for sure.

Interestingly enough, throughout history, animals (*19. help, often*) _____ people to predict earthquakes shortly before they happen. At present, some scientists (*20. study*) _____ catfish because catfish swim excitedly just before an earthquake. According to some studies, snakes, monkeys, and rodents (*21. appear, also*)_____ _____ to be sensitive to the approach of violent movement in the earth's surface. Some animals seem to know a great deal more than humans about when an earthquake will occur.

In recent years, scientists (*22. develop*) _____ many extremely sensitive instruments. Perhaps someday the instruments (*23. give*) _____ us a sufficiently early warning so that we can be waiting calmly in a safe place when the next earthquake (*24. strike*) _____.

◇ **PRACTICE 44—SELFSTUDY: Error analysis. (Chapter 1)**

Directions: Find and correct the errors in the following sentences. All of the mistakes are in verb tense form and usage.

1. I am studying here since last January.

2. By the time I return to my country, I am away from home for more than three years.

3. As soon as I will graduate, I going to return to my hometown.

4. By the end of the 21st century, scientists will had discovered the cure for the common cold.

5. I want to get married, but I don't meet the right person yet.

6. I have been seeing that movie three times, and now I am wanting to see it again.

7. Last night, I have had dinner with two friends. I knew both of them for a long time.

8. I am not like my job at the restaurant. My brother wants me to change it. I am thinking he is right.

9. So far this week, the teachers are giving us a lot of homework every day.

10. There are fewer than 40 presidents of the United States since it became a country. George Washington had been the first president. He was become the president in 1789.

11. Mr. Sellers was just getting off the plane when he feels a sharp pain in his chest.

12. When I got home to my apartment last night, I use my key to open the door as usual. But the door didn't open. I trying my key again and again with no luck. So I am knocking on the door for my wife to let me in. Finally the door opens, but I don't saw my wife on the other side. I saw a stranger. I had been try to get into the wrong apartment! I quickly apologizing and am went to my own apartment.

◇ PRACTICE TEST A—SELFSTUDY: Verb tenses. (Chapter 1)

Directions: Choose the correct answer.
Example:

__C__ *I've been in this city for a long time. I _____ here sixteen years ago.*
      A. have come   *B. was coming*   *C. came*   *D. had come*

_____ 1. "Hurry up! We're waiting for you. What's taking you so long?"
    "I _____ for an important phone call. Go ahead and leave without me."
    A. wait   B. will wait   C. am waiting   D. have waited.

_____ 2. "Robert is going to be famous someday. He _____ in three movies already."
    "I'm sure he'll be a star."
    A. has been appearing   B. had appeared
    C. has appeared   D. appeared

_____ 3. "Where's Polly?"
    "She _____."
    A. is in her room studying   B. in her room is studying
    C. studies in her room   D. has in her room studied

_____ 4. "Hello? Alice? This is Jeff. How are you?"
    "Jeff? What a coincidence! I _____ about you when the phone rang."
    A. was just thinking   B. just thought
    C. have just been thinking   D. was just thought

_____ 5. "What _____ about the new simplified tax law?"
    "It's more confusing than the old one."
    A. are you thinking   B. do you think
    C. have you thought   D. have you been thinking

_____ 6. "When is Mr. Fields planning to retire?"
    "Soon, I think. He _____ here for a long time. He'll probably retire either next year or the year after that."
    A. worked   B. had been working
    C. has been working   D. is working

_C_ 7. "Why did you buy all this sugar and chocolate?"
"I _____ a delicious dessert for dinner tonight."
    A. make   B. will make
    C. am going to make   D. will have made

_C_ 8. "Let's go! What's taking you so long?"
"I'll be there as soon as I _____ my keys."
    A. found   B. will find   C. find   D. am finding

_B_ 9. Next week when there _____ a full moon, the ocean tides will be higher.
    A. is being   B. is   C. will be   D. will have been

_C_ 10. While I _____ TV last night, a mouse ran across the floor.
    A. watch   B. watched   C. was watching   D. am watching

_A_ 11. Fish were among the earliest forms of life. Fish _____ on earth for ages and ages.
    A. existed   B. are existing   C. exist   D. have existed

_A_ 12. The phone _____ constantly since Jack announced his candidacy for president this morning.
    A. has been ringing   B. rang
    C. had rung   D. had been ringing

_D_ 13. The earth _____ on the sun for its heat and light.
    A. is depend   B. depending   C. has depend   D. depends

_A_ 14. I don't feel good. I _____ home from work tomorrow.
    A. am staying   B. stay
    C. will have stayed   D. stayed

_B_ 15. Today there are weather satellites that beam down information about the earth's atmosphere. In the last two decades, space exploration _____ great contributions to weather forecasting.
    A. is making   B. has made   C. made   D. makes

_B_ 16. On July 20, 1969, Astronaut Neil Armstrong _____ down onto the moon, the first person ever to set foot on another celestial body.
    A. was stepping   B. stepped   C. has stepped   D. was step

_D_ 17. The plane's departure was delayed because of mechanical difficulties. When the weary passengers finally boarded the aircraft, many were annoyed and irritable because they _____ in the airport for three and a half hours.
    A. are waiting   B. were waiting
    C. have been waiting   D. had been waiting

_B_ 18. If coastal erosion continues to take place at the present rate, in another fifty years this beach _____ anymore.
    A. doesn't exist   B. isn't going to exist
    C. isn't existing   D. won't be existing

_D_ 19. Homestead High School's football team _____ a championship until last season, when the new coach led them to take first place in their league.
    A. has never won   B. is never winning
    C. had never been winning   D. had never won

_C_ 20. To be able to qualify as an interpreter, many years of intensive language study are required for non-native speakers. By the end of this year, Chen _____ English for three years, but he will still need more training and experience before he masters the language.
    A. will be studying   B. has studied
    C. will have been studying   D. has been studying

Directions: Choose the correct answer.

Example:

__*C*__ *I've been in this city for a long time. I _____ here sixteen years ago.*
     A. have come   *B. was coming*   *C. came*   *D. had come*

_____ 1. "May I speak to Dr. Paine, please?"
     "I'm sorry, he _____ a patient at the moment. Can I help you?"
     A. is seeing   B. sees
     C. has been seeing   D. was seeing

_____ 2. "When are you going to ask your boss for a raise?"
     "_____ to her twice already! I don't think she wants to give me one."
     A. I've talked   B. I've been talking
     C. I was talking   D. I'd talked

_____ 3. "Do you think Harry will want something to eat after he gets here?"
     "I hope not. It'll probably be after midnight, and we _____."
     A. are sleeping   B. will be sleeping
     C. have been sleeping   D. be sleeping

_____ 4. "Paul, could you please turn off the stove? The potatoes _____ for at least thirty minutes."
     "I can't. I'm feeding the baby."
     A. are boiling   B. boiling
     C. have been boiling   D. were boiling

_____ 5. "Is it true that spaghetti didn't originate in Italy?"
     "Yes. The Chinese _____ spaghetti dishes for a long time before Marco Polo brought it back to Italy."
     A. have been making   B. have made
     C. had been making   D. make

_____ 6. "I once saw a turtle that had wings. The turtle flew into the air to catch insects."
     "Stop kidding. I _____ you!"
     A. don't believe   B. am not believing
     C. didn't believe   D. wasn't believing

_____ 7. "Could someone help me lift the lawnmower into the pickup truck?"
     "I'm not busy. I _____ you."
     "Thanks."
     A. help   B. will help
     C. am going to help   D. am helping

_____ 8. My family loves this house. It _____ the family home ever since my grandfather built it 60 years ago.
     A. was   B. has been   C. is   D. will be

_____ 9. Here's an interesting statistic: On a typical day, the average person _____ about 48,000 words. How many words did you speak today?
     A. spoke   B. was speaking   C. speaks   D. is speaking

_____ 10. I know you feel bad now, Tommy, but try to put it out of your mind. By the time you're an adult, you _____ all about it.
     A. forget   B. will have forgotten
     C. will be forgetting   D. forgot

_____ 11. It's against the law to kill the black rhinoceros. They _____ extinct.
     A. became   B. have become   C. become   D. are becoming

_____ 12. After ten unhappy years, Janice finally quit her job. She _____ along with her boss for a long time before she finally decided to look for a new position.
    A. hadn't been getting   B. isn't getting
    C. didn't get   D. hasn't been getting

_____ 13. The National Hurricane Center is closely watching a strong hurricane over the Atlantic Ocean. When it _____ the coast of Texas sometime tomorrow afternoon, it will bring with it great destructive force.
    A. reaches   B. will reach   C. is reaching   D. reaching

_____ 14. At one time, huge prehistoric reptiles dominated the earth. This Age of Dinosaurs _____ much longer than the present Age of Mammals has lasted to date.
    A. lasted   B. was lasting   C. has lasted   D. had lasted

_____ 15. Jim, why don't you take some time off? You _____ too hard lately. Take a short vacation.
    A. worked   B. work
    C. were working   D. have been working

_____ 16. The city is rebuilding its dilapidated waterfront, transforming it into a pleasant and fashionable outdoor mall. Next summer when the tourists arrive, they _____ 104 beautiful new shops and restaurants in the area where the old run-down waterfront properties used to stand.
    A. will found   B. will be finding
    C. will have found   D. will find

_____ 17. A minor earthquake occurred at 2:07 A.M. on January 3. Most of the people in the village _____ at the time and didn't even know it had occurred until the next morning.
    A. slept   B. had slept   C. were sleeping   D. sleep

_____ 18. The little girl started to cry. She _____ her doll, and no one was able to find it for her.
    A. has lost   B. had lost   C. was losing   D. was lost

_____ 19. According to research reports, people usually _____ in their sleep 25 to 30 times each night.
    A. turn   B. are turning   C. have turned   D. turned

_____ 20. Jane's eyes burned and her shoulders ached. She _____ at the computer for 5 straight hours. Finally, she took a break.
    A. is sitting   B. has been sitting
    C. was sitting   D. had been sitting

CHAPTER *2*
Modal Auxiliaries and Similar Expressions

◇ **PRACTICE 1—SELFSTUDY: Verb forms with modal auxiliaries. (Chart 2-1)**

Directions: Choose the correct completion.

__*C*__ 1. Mary can _____ to the meeting.
A. comes   B. to come   C. come

_____ 2. Jack should _____ harder.
A. studies   B. to study   C. study

_____ 3. The whole team must _____ together in order to win the game.
A. worked   B. to work   C. work

_____ 4. We ought _____ before we drop in on Peter and Marcia. They may be busy.
A. called   B. to call   C. call

_____ 5. Paul can _____ Chinese very well because he studied it for six years.
A. speaks   B. to speak   C. speak

_____ 6. May I _____ you?
A. can help   B. to help   C. help

_____ 7. The construction crew might _____ the bridge in time for the holiday traffic.
A. finished   B. to finish   C. finish

_____ 8. We had better _____ an umbrella when we go out. It looks like it's going to rain.
A. taken   B. to take   C. take

_____ 9. I couldn't _____ that book because I didn't bring any money with me.
A. bought   B. to buy   C. buy

_____ 10. The children should _____ "thank you" to you when you gave them their gifts.
A. has said   B. to have said   C. have said

_____ 11. Tom could _____ us to help him move.
A. had asked   B. to have asked   C. have asked

_____ 12. I can't find the grocery list. Gail must _____ it with her when she went out.
A. has taken   B. to have taken   C. have taken

◇ **PRACTICE 2—SELFSTUDY: Making polite requests. (Charts 2-2 → 2-5)**

Directions: Change the following sentences into polite requests using the words in parentheses.

   1. I want you to hand me that book. (*would*)

     → *Would you please hand me that book?*

   2. I want you to give me some advice about buying a computer. (*could*)

   3. I want to borrow your wheelbarrow. (*could*)

   4. I want to have a cup of coffee. (*may*)

   5. I want to use your bicycle tomorrow. (*can*)

   6. I want you to read over my composition for spelling errors. (*would*)

   7. I want you to open the door for me. (*would you mind*)

   8. I want to leave early. (*would you mind*)

◇ **PRACTICE 3—SELFSTUDY: Using *would you mind*. (Chart 2-4)**

Directions: Using the verb in parentheses, fill in the blank either with *if I* + the PAST tense or with the *-ing* form of the verb, as appropriate.

   1. A: It's hot in here. Would you mind (*open*) ___***opening***___ the window?

      B: Not at all. I'd be glad to.

   2. A: It's hot in here. Would you mind (*open*) ___***if I opened***___ the window?

      B: Not at all. Go right ahead. I think it's hot in here, too.

   3. A: Would you mind (*take*) _____ the book back to the library for me?

      B: Not at all.

   4. A: This story you wrote is really good. Would you mind (*show*) _____ it to my English teacher?

      B: Go right ahead. That'd be fine.

   5. A: I'll wash the dishes. Would you mind (*dry*) _____ them. That would help me a lot.

      B: I'd be happy to.

   6. A: I'm feeling kind of tired and worn out. This heavy work in the hot sun is hard on me. Would you mind (*finish*) _____ the work by yourself?

      B: No problem, Grandpa. Why don't you go in and rest? I'll finish it up.

   7. A: Would you mind (*use*) _____ your name as a reference on this job application?

      B: Not at all. In fact, ask them to call me.

   8. A: Would you mind (*wait*) _____ here for just a minute? I need to run back to the classroom. I forgot my notebook.

      B: Sure. Go ahead. I'll wait right here.

9. A: You have an atlas, don't you? Would you mind (*borrow*) _____ it for a

   minute? I need to settle an argument. My friend says Timbuktu is in Asia, and I say it's in

   Australia.

   B: You're both wrong. It's in Africa. Here's the atlas. Look it up for yourself.

10. A: Since this is the first time you've owned a computer, would you mind (*give*) _____

   _____ you some advice?

   B: Not at all. I'd appreciate it.

◇ **PRACTICE 4—GUIDED STUDY: Imperatives. (Chart 2-5)**

Directions: Complete the sentences with an appropriate verb (affirmative or negative) in the following. All of the sentences are imperative. Use *please* if the sentence is a polite request.

1. _____***Look***_____ out! A car is coming.

2. ___***Please wait***___ for me. I'll be ready in just a few minutes.

3. ___***Don't tell***___ anyone my secret. Do you promise?

4. _____ me the salt and pepper.

5. _____ up! It's time to get up.

6. _____ that pot! It's hot. You'll burn yourself.

7. _____ busy! We don't have all day.

8. _____ carefully to my directions. I'll say them only once.

9. _____ pages 35 through 70 for tomorrow's class.

10. _____ it easy. There's no need to get angry.

11. _____ the window.

12. _____ ! I can hear you. You don't have to yell.

13. _____ this soup. It's delicious.

14. _____ me in front of the bookstore at three o'clock.

15. _____ ! I'm drowning.

16. _____ the light on. It's getting dark in here.

17. _____ a newspaper on your way home.

18. _____ it over for a few days. You don't have to make a decision now.

19. _____ to bring a No. 2 pencil to the test. You will need one.

20. _____ here tomorrow at nine o'clock.

◇ **PRACTICE 5—GUIDED STUDY: Making polite requests. (Charts 2-2 → 2-5)**

Directions: Complete the polite requests in the following with your own words. Try to imagine what the speaker might say in the given situation.

1.   WAITER: Good evening. Are you ready to order?

   CUSTOMER: No, we're not. Could . . . ?   (→ *Could we have a few more minutes?*)

   WAITER: Certainly. And if you have any questions, I'd be happy to tell you about anything on the menu.

2.   JACK: What's the trouble officer?
    OFFICER: You made an illegal U-turn.
    JACK: I did?
    OFFICER: Yes. May...?
    JACK: Certainly. It's in my wallet.
    OFFICER: Would you please remove it from your wallet?

3.   SALLY: Are you driving to the meeting tonight?
    MIKE: Un-huh, I am.
    SALLY: Could...?
    MIKE: Sure. I'll pick you up at 7:00.

4.   MECHANIC: What seems to be the trouble with your car?
    CUSTOMER: Something's wrong with the brakes, I think. Could...?
    MECHANIC: Sure. Just pull the car into the garage.

5.   MR. PENN: Something's come up, and I can't meet with you Tuesday. Would you mind...?
    MS. GRAY: Let me check my calendar.

6.   TOM: I've never been to your house. Will...?
    MARY: That won't be necessary. Al said that he would drive by and pick you up.

7.   CLERK: May...?
    CUSTOMER: Yes, please. Could...?
    CLERK: Surely. What sort of slacks are you interested in?

8.   ART: Are you enjoying the movie?
    IRIS: Yes, but I can't see over the man sitting in front of me. Would you mind...?
    ART: Not at all. I see two empty seats across the aisle.

9.   CARLO: I have to leave now, but I'd like to continue this conversation later. Could...?
    ANNE: Of course. My phone number is 555-1716. I'll look forward to hearing from you.

10.   MOTHER: The baby is trying to sleep. Would...?
    SON: But Mom! I've been waiting all evening to watch this show!
    MOTHER: Well, all right, but could...?
    SON: Okay.

◇ **PRACTICE 6—GUIDED STUDY: Making polite requests. (Charts 2-4 → 2-5)**

Directions: For the given situation, make up a short dialogue between two speakers. The dialogue should contain a polite request and a response to that request.

Example: You don't have enough money to go to a movie tonight. You want to borrow some from your roommate.

Possible Dialogue:
    ME: There's a movie I really want to see tonight, but I'm running a little low on money right now. Could I borrow a few dollars? I'll pay you back Friday.
MY ROOMMATE: Sure. No problem. How much do you need?

1. Your roommate is making a sandwich and it looks delicious. You'd like to have one, but you don't feel like going to the trouble of making one yourself.

2. You are in a fast-food restaurant and want to sit down to eat your lunch. The only empty seat you can see is at a table where three people are eating and are having a lively conversation.

3. You can't get your car started and you will soon be late for work. Your neighbor is backing out of his driveway and waves at you. You shout at him to stop and ask him for help.

4. Paul just arrived at work and remembered that he left the stove burner on under the coffee pot back in his apartment. His neighbor Jack has a key to the front door, and Paul knows that Jack hasn't left for work yet. Anxiously, he telephones Jack for help.

5. A man and a woman are having dinner in a restaurant and discussing business. The man gets up and bumps the table, spilling a plate of food onto the woman's lap. He needs help from the waiter standing nearby.

6. You have to write a research paper for your biology class. You have never used the library and don't know how to find the books you need. You need assistance from the librarian.

7. Carol and Larry are going out for the evening. They are in a hurry and don't have time to give the children baths and get them ready for bed. They would like the babysitter to do this.

8. You had been driving along the highway when suddenly you had a flat tire, so you pulled over to the shoulder and stopped the car. You opened the trunk and discovered that you had no jack and couldn't change the tire. A car pulled up behind you, and a man got out and asked if you needed help.

9. You need help in understanding some of the problems in your physics class, and your friend is the best student in the class. Likewise, she needs help in preparing for her German exam, and you are the best student in the German class. You need to work out an arrangement together.

◇ **PRACTICE 7—SELFSTUDY:** *Must (not)* and *(do not) have to.* (Charts 2-6 and 2-7)

Directions: Choose the correct completion according to the meaning.

_____ 1. Soldiers __B__ disobey a superior officer.
  A. must/have to   B. must not   C. don't have to

_____ 2. To stay alive, people _____ breathe oxygen.
  A. must/have to   B. must not   C. don't have to

_____ 3. You _____ finish your work on this project before you go on vacation. You'll probably lose your job if you don't.
  A. must/have to   B. must not   C. don't have to

_____ 4. If you have an aquarium, you _____ give your tropical fish too much food or they'll die.
  A. must/have to   B. must not   C. don't have to

_____ 5. To be a successful mountain climber, you _____ have a great deal of stamina.
A. must/have to   B. must not   C. don't have to

_____ 6. Thank goodness we _____ eat fish again tonight. Dad didn't catch any today.
A. must/have to   B. must not   C. don't have to

_____ 7. You _____ exert yourself. You're still not fully recovered from your surgery.
A. must/have to   B. must not   C. don't have to

_____ 8. My room is a mess, but I _____ clean it before I go out tonight. I can do it in the morning.
A. must/have to   B. must not   C. don't have to

_____ 9. We really _____ help Marge move to her new apartment over the weekend. Not only is it too difficult for one person, but she still has her arm in a sling from her shoulder sprain a week ago.
A. must/have to   B. must not   C. don't have to

_____ 10. Bill is in the darkroom developing the negatives of the photos he took on his last trip to Peru. You _____ open the door while he's there because the light will ruin the pictures.
A. must/have to   B. must not   C. don't have to

◇ **PRACTICE 8—SELFSTUDY:** *Have to*, verb form review. (Charts 2-6 and 2-7)

Directions: Complete the sentences with any appropriate form of **have to**. Include any words in parentheses.

1. A: (You) __***Do you have to***__ leave so early?

   B: I'm afraid I do. I have some work I __***have to***__ finish before I go to bed tonight.

2. Last night Jack __***had to***__ go to a meeting. (You) __***Did you have to***__ go to the meeting last night too?

3. Joan travels to the Soviet Union frequently. Luckily, she speaks Russian, so she (*not*)

   _____ rely on an interpreter when she's there.

4. I (*not*) _____ water the garden later today. Joe has agreed to do it for me.

5. I _____ write three term papers since the beginning of the semester.

6. Why (*Tom*) _____ leave work early yesterday?

7. I found some milk in the refrigerator, so we (*not*) _____ go to the store after all. There is plenty.

8. (*John*) _____ buy a round-trip ticket when he went to Egypt?

9. Matt is nearsighted. He _____ wear glasses ever since he was ten years old.

10. By the time this week is finished, I _____ take eight examinations in five days. The life of a student isn't easy!

11. (*You, not*) _____ return these books to the library today? Aren't they due?

12. If Jean stays in Brazil much longer, she _____ teach English part-time so that she'll have enough money to support herself. (*She*) _____ _____ apply for a special work visa? Or can she work part-time on a student visa?

13. Because it was Emily's birthday yesterday, she (*not*) _____ do any of her regular chores, and her mother let her choose anything she wanted to eat for dinner.

14. When I arrived in Rome last week, I was looking forward to practicing my Italian. I'm disappointed because I (*not*) _____ speak Italian very much at all since I got here. Everyone keeps talking to me in English.

◇ **PRACTICE 9—GUIDED STUDY:** *Should, ought to, had better.* (Chart 2-8)

Directions: Give advice to the people in the following situations. Use *should, ought to,* or *had better*.

1. Ann would like to make some new friends. → *I think she should join some clubs so she can meet people who have similar interests.*
2. Ellen is having a lot of trouble in her chemistry class. She's failed the last two tests.
3. Sam and Tim, both teenagers, have messed up the house, and their parents are coming home soon.
4. Pierre is feeling really homesick these days.
5. Ron is wearing jeans. He's expected at a formal reception this evening.
6. Alice is planning to drive across country by herself this summer, but she's never changed a flat tire or even pumped her own gas.
7. Mike can't understand what's going on in his English class.
8. William's parents expect him to work in the family business, a shoe store, but he wants to be an architect.
9. Pam's younger brother, who is 18, is using illegal drugs. How can she help him?
10. Richard's roommate stays up very late studying. While his roommate is studying, he listens to loud music, and Richard can't get to sleep.
11. The Taylors' daughter is very excited about going to Denmark to live and study for four months. You've been an international student, haven't you? Could you give her some advice?
12. Virginia doesn't really have enough money saved for a vacation, but she wants to go someplace. Do you know of any inexpensive but wonderful place she could go?
13. Mr. Rice is behind schedule in the history class he's teaching. Should he skip some less important historical events, or should he give the students longer assignments?
14. Maria is expecting George to meet her when she arrives at the airport in an hour, but George's car won't start. What should George do?

◇ **PRACTICE 10—GUIDED STUDY:** *Should, ought to, had better.* (Chart 2-8)

Directions: Complete the following dialogues with your own words.

1. A: Oops! I spilled _____ *coffee on my shirt.* _____

   B: You'd better _____ *change shirts before you go to your job interview.* _____

2. A: Lately I can't seem to concentrate on anything, and I feel _____

   B: Maybe you should _____

3. A: The shoes I bought last week _____

   B: Oh? You ought to _____

4. A: Jimmy, you'd better _____ or I'm going to
   _____

   B: Okay, Mom. I'll do it right now.

5. A: I'd better _____

   B: I agree. It'll be winter soon.

6. A: I've been studying for three days straight.

   B: I know. You should _____

   A: I know, but _____

7. A: Kids, your dad and I work hard all day long. Don't you think you should _____

   _____

   B: _____

8. A: My doctor said I should _____, but I _____

   B: Well, I think you'd better _____ _____

9. A: Mary's always wanted to learn how to _____

   B: Isn't your brother _____

   You should _____

10. A: Have you _____

    B: No, not yet.

    A: You really ought to _____

11. A: You should _____ if you _____

    B: Thanks for reminding me. I'd better _____

12. A: Do you think I ought to _____ or _____

    B: I think you'd better _____. If you don't, _____

    _____

◇ PRACTICE 11—GUIDED STUDY: The past form of *should*. (Chart 2-9)

Directions: Discuss or write what you think the people in the following situations ***should have done*** and ***should not have done***.

1. Tom didn't study for the test. During the exam he panicked and started looking at other students' test papers. He didn't think the teacher saw him, but she did. She warned him once to stop cheating, but he continued. As a result, the teacher took Tom's test paper, told him to leave the room, and failed him on the exam.

   Tom should have studied for the test.
   He shouldn't have panicked during the test.
   He shouldn't have started cheating.
   He should have known the teacher would see him cheating.
   He should have stopped cheating after the first warning.
   The teacher should have ripped up Tom's paper and sent him out of the room the first time she
   *   saw him cheating.*

2. John and his wife, Julie, had good jobs as professionals in New York City. John was offered a high paying job in Chicago, which he immediately accepted. Julie was shocked when he came home that evening and told her the news. She liked her job and the people she worked with, and she did not want to move away and look for another job.

3. Ann agreed to meet her friend Carl at the library to help him with his chemistry homework. On the way, she stopped at a cafe where her boyfriend worked. Her boyfriend told her he could get off work early that night, so the two of them decided to go to a movie. Ann didn't cancel her plans with Carl. Carl waited for three hours at the library.

4. Joe was unemployed. He was desperately sad because he had no money to buy a birthday gift for his son, so he stole a bicycle from the park to give to his son. His son recognized the bike as one that belonged to a friend of his. The son refused to accept the stolen gift and was so angry that he would no longer speak to his father.

5. Donna had been saving her money for three years for a trip abroad. Her brother Larry had a good job but spent all of his money on expensive cars, clothes, and entertainment. Suddenly, Larry was fired from his job and had no money to support himself while he looked for another one. Donna lent him nearly all of her savings, and within three weeks he spent it all on his car, more clothes, and expensive restaurants.

6. Sarah often exaggerated and once told a co-worker that she was fluent in French even though she had studied only a little and could not really communicate in the language. A few days later, her boss asked her to come to his office to interpret a meeting with a French businessman who had just arrived from Paris to negotiate a major contract with the company. After an embarrassed silence, Sarah told her boss that she was feeling ill and had to go home immediately.

7. Jack discovered that ten dollars was missing from his wallet. He confronted his two sons, Mark and Jason, and found a ten-dollar bill in Jason's shirt pocket. Jack became angry, sent Jason to his room, and grounded him for a week. Mark simply walked outside, but felt very bad because he was the one who had taken the money. Jason had found out and was trying to return it to his father's wallet so that Mark wouldn't get in trouble.

◇ PRACTICE 12—GUIDED STUDY: *Be to.* (Chart 2-10)

Directions: Pretend you are taking a bus load of students (ages 12 to 16) on a trip to a nearby town. You are the supervisor. Make a list of rules you want the students to follow. Use *be to* in your list.

1. You don't want the students to bring glass containers onto the bus. → *For safety reasons, students are not to bring glass containers (e.g., pop bottles) onto the bus.*
2. You want the students to keep the bus clean.
3. You don't want the students to lean out of the windows.
4. You don't want the students to toss anything from the bus.
5. You want the students to store personal items under the seats.
6. You don't want the students to yell, scream, or shout on the bus.
7. You want the students to stay in their seats at all times while the bus is moving.
8. (*Make additional rules you want the students to follow.*)

◇ **PRACTICE 13—GUIDED STUDY:** Necessity, advisability, and expectations. (Charts 2-6 → 2-10)

Directions: Choose one of the following topics for writing. Use the given words and expressions.

Words and expressions to use:

a. should
b. have to
c. be supposed to
d. shouldn't
e. be to
f. be not supposed to

g. had better
h. must
i. ought to
j. must not
k. do not have to
l. have got to

Topics:

1. Pretend that you are the supervisor of a roomful of young children. The children are in your care for the next six hours. What would you say to them to make sure they understand your expectations and your rules so that they will be safe and cooperative?

   a. *You should pick up your toys when you are finished playing with them.*
   b. *You have to stay in this room. Do not go outside without my permission.*
   c. *You're supposed to take a short nap at one o'clock.*
   d. *etc.*

2. Pretend that you are the supervisor of salesclerks in a large department store and that you are talking to two new employees. You want to acquaint them with their job and your expectations.

3. Pretend that you are a travel agent and you are helping two students who are traveling to your country/your hometown for a vacation. You want them to understand some customs as well as practical travel arrangements.

4. Pretend that you are instructing the babysitter who will watch your three children, all under the age of ten, while you are out for the evening. They haven't had dinner, and they don't like to go to bed when they're told to.

5. Pretend that you are teaching your younger sister how to drive a car. This is her first time behind the wheel, and she knows little about driving regulations and the operation of an automobile.

◇ **PRACTICE 14—GUIDED STUDY:** *Let's, why don't, shall I/we.* (Chart 2-11)

Directions: Complete the dialogues with your own words.

1. A: There's a new Japanese restaurant that just opened downtown. Let's _____ *eat there* _____ *tonight.* _____.

   B: Great idea. I'd like some good sushi.

   A: Why don't _____ *you call and make a reservation?* _____ Make it for about 7:30.

   B: No, let's _____ *make it for 8:00.* _____ I'll be working until 7:30 tonight.

2. A: I don't feel like staying home today.

   B: Neither do I. Why don't _____

   A: Hey, that's a great idea! What time shall _____

   B: How about in an hour?

   A: Good.

3. A: We'll never find an apartment we can afford in the middle of the city. Why don't

   _____

   It's farther, but the apartments are probably less expensive.

   B: Okay. I'll drive. Let's _____

   A: We should look in the classified ads for that area. Why don't _____

   B: Good idea. Here, I have some change.

4. A: Shall _____ or _____ first?

   B: Let's _____ first, then we can take our time over dinner.

   A: Why don't _____

   B: Yes. Then we'll be sure _____

5. A: Let's _____ over the weekend. The fresh

   air would do us both good.

   B: I agree. Why don't _____

   A: No. Sleeping in a tent is too uncomfortable. Let's _____

   It won't be that expensive, and we'll have hot water and a TV in the room. All the

   comforts of home.

6. A: How are we ever going to prepare for tomorrow's exam? There's so much to know!

   B: Why don't _____

   A: All right. And then let's _____

   B: Okay, but after that we should _____

7. A: I think it's time for us to do something to fix up the apartment.

   B: Okay. Why don't _____

   A: That's a good idea. Shall _____

   B: Why not?

   A: Well then, why don't you _____ And I'll _____

   B: Well, I'd really like to help, but I have to get back to my work.

8. A: I'm worried about Barbara. She's never this late.

   B: Let's not _____ She's probably just held up in traffic.

   A: Why don't _____

   At least then we'll know if she left there on time.

   B: Okay, if it'll make you feel better, but why don't _____

   I'm sure she's okay.

9. A: This pasta is delicious! Why don't _____

   B: No, thank you. I'm full. Let's _____

   A: What? No dessert? This place is famous for its pies.

   B: I couldn't eat another bite, but I'll wait for you. Shall _____

   A: Yes, if you see him. He hasn't been back since he brought our dinner.

Directions: For each of the following situations, give three suggestions with ***could***. Then give definite advice with ***should***.

1. It's late at night. Tony is home by himself. He hears a window break. He thinks it's a burglar. Now what? What could or should he do now?
    → *He **could** hide under his bed. He **could** run to the phone and call the police. He **could** pick up his baseball bat and go looking for the intruder.*
    → *He **should** leave the house and go to his neighbor's house to call the police.*

2. You and your family are driving in the countryside, and you notice that you are almost out of gas. You manage to make it to a small town nearby and discover that the only gas station in town is closed. Now what? (*We could . . . . We could . . . . We could . . . . We should . . . .*)

3. Kim is an insomniac. She tosses and turns until 2 or 3 A.M. every night. She watches television, reads books, and listens to the radio, but nothing seems to help. It's beginning to affect her work, as she has to be in her office at 8:00 A.M. She's always tired. She needs some advice.

4. Al has invited his boss out for dinner at an expensive restaurant. The food was delicious, and they're having a final cup of coffee when the waiter brings the bill. Al reaches in his pocket and discovers that he's left his wallet at home. He fumbles nervously and breaks out in a cold sweat. Now what?

5. Bruce has helped his mother onto the train and escorted her to a seat. While he is saying goodbye, the train begins pulling away from the station. By the time he gets through the crowded aisles to the exit, the train is traveling fast. Now what?

◇ PRACTICE 16—SELFSTUDY: Degrees of certainty: *must* and *may/might/could*. (Chart 2-13)

Directions: Which of the two completions is the speaker most likely to say? Choose the best completion.

__*B*__   1. "Do you know where Mary is?"
           "She _____ be at home. She was going either there or to Barbara's after work."
           A. must   B. could

_A_   2. "Look at all the children waiting for the bus. What time is it?"
"It _____ be after 3:00. That's when school is out."
     A.   must   B.   might

_A_   3. "I heard that Jose has received a scholarship and will be able to attend the university in the fall."
"Wonderful! He _____ be very happy to have the matter finally settled."
     A.   must   B.   may

_B_   4. "Excuse me. Could you tell me which bus I should take to get to City Hall?"
"Bus number 63 _____ go there. But maybe you'd better ask the driver."
     A.   must   B.   might

_____   5. "George says that we're going to have a very high inflation rate next year."
"He _____ be right. I think his view is as good as anybody's. I've heard strong opinions on all sides of that issue."
     A.   must   B.   could

_____   6. "Do you suppose Carl is sick?"
"He _____ be. Nothing else would have kept him from coming to this meeting."
     A.   must   B.   may

_____   7. "Have you heard anything from Ed? Is he still in Africa?"
"He _____ be, or he _____ already be on his way home. I'm just not sure."
     A.   must/must   B.   could/could

_____   8. "Is that a famous person over there in the middle of that crowd?"
"It _____ be. Everyone's trying to get her autograph."
     A.   must   B.   might

_____   9. "Isn't Peter Reeves a banker?"
"Yes. Why don't you talk to him? He _____ be able to help you with your loan."
     A.   must   B.   may

_____   10. "Isn't Margaret's daughter over sixteen?"
"She _____ be. I saw her driving a car, and you have to be at least sixteen to get a driver's license."
     A.   must   B.   might

_____   11. "Is that Bob's brother standing with him in the cafeteria line?"
"It _____ be, I suppose. It does look a little like him."
     A.   must   B.   could

_____   12. "Overall, don't you think the possibility of world peace is greater now than ever before?"
"It _____ be. I don't know. Political relationships can be fragile."
     A.   must   B.   may

◇ **PRACTICE 17—GUIDED STUDY:**   Degrees of certainty: *must* and *may/might/could.*
                            (Chart 2-13)

Directions: Which of the following completions would the speaker probably say? Choose the best completion.

_**A**_   1. "Is Jeff a good student?"
"He _____. Although he seems to study very little, I heard he was offered a scholarship for next year."
     A.   must be   B.   could be   C.   is

_____ 2. "The speedometer on my car is broken."
"Do you think you're driving over the speed limit?"
"I don't know. I _____."
    A. must be   B. might be   C. am

_____ 3. "You've been on the go all day. Aren't you exhausted?"
"Yes, I _____. I can't remember when I've ever been this worn out."
    A. must be   B. may be   C. am

_____ 4. "Do you think the grocery store is still open?"
"It _____. I can't ever remember what their hours are."
    A. must be   B. could be   C. is

_____ 5. "Have you seen the new movie playing at the Bijou?"
"No, but it _____ sad. Many people leaving the theater seem to have been crying."
    A. must be   B. might be   C. is

_____ 6. "Where's the chicken we had left over from dinner last night?"
"I just saw it when I got some ice cubes. It _____ in the freezer."
    A. must be   B. might be   C. is

_____ 7. "It's supposed to rain tomorrow."
"I know, but the forecast _____ wrong. Weather forecasts are far from 100% accurate."
    A. must be   B. could be   C. is

_____ 8. "Do you hear that squeak? What is it?"
"I don't know. It _____ a mouse. Isn't that what a mouse sounds like?"
    A. must be   B. may be   C. is

_____ 9. "How old do you think Roger is?"
"I just looked at his driver's license. He _____ 33."
    A. must be   B. could be   C. is

_____ 10. "Is China the largest country in the world, or is it Brazil?"
"Neither. It _____ the Soviet Union. It has nearly three times the area of either China or Brazil."
    A. must be   B. might be   C. is

◇ **PRACTICE 18—GUIDED STUDY:** **Making conclusions: _must_ and _must not_.**
                                         (Charts 2-13 → 2-15)

Directions: Make logical conclusions about the following situations. Use _**must**_ or _**must not**_ for your "best guess."

1. The Adams' house is dark and quiet. Their car isn't in the driveway.
   → _They must not be at home._

2. We had a test in class yesterday. Charles, who rarely studies and usually fails the tests, got a score of 95% this time.
   → _He must have studied for the test._

3. The man sitting behind us has been talking throughout the movie. He knows what's going to happen before it happens.

4. Anita is in bed. The lights are out, and I can hear her snoring.

5. Mrs. Jenkins has lost some of her hearing. Yesterday the children asked her several times for some cookies, but she didn't answer.

6. Everyone who had the fish for dinner at that restaurant last night got sick. Those who didn't eat the fish were fine.

7. Jeremy's car radio is always set on the classical music station. He also keeps a supply of classical music tapes in the car.

8. When Jeremy's wife is in the car with him, she always asks him to change the station or the tape.

9. Diane never seems to have enough money. I tried to call her last night and got a recording telling me that her phone had been disconnected.

10. I hear sirens and see two fire trucks speeding down the street.

11. Janet described the Eiffel Tower to some of her friends and showed them some photographs she had taken.

12. Four people had dinner together. Two of them ate wild mushrooms, and two of them didn't. The two who ate the mushrooms are now critically ill.

◇ PRACTICE 19—GUIDED STUDY: Degrees of certainty: *must*. (Charts 2-13 → 2-15)

Directions: Look around yourself right now and make some ''best guesses'' using *must* about objects, people, sounds, smells, etc. Write what you see or hear, and then make a logical conclusion.

Examples:

My roommate's books are on his bed. He must have come back from class and then left again.
My wife is reading a letter and smiling. The letter must contain some good news.
I hear a dog barking. It must be Rover, my neighbor's dog.

◇ PRACTICE 20—SELFSTUDY: Degrees of certainty. (Charts 2-13 → 2-16)

Directions: Using the information about the given situation, complete the sentences.

1. *Situation:*   Someone's knocking at the door. I wonder who it is.
   Information: **Tom** is out of town.
   Fred called a half an hour ago, and said he wanted to stop by this afternoon.
   Alice is a neighbor who sometimes drops by in the middle of the day.

   a. It must be _____*Fred*_____.

   b. It couldn't be _____*Tom*_____.

   c. I suppose it might be _____*Alice*_____.

2. *Situation:*   Someone ran into the tree in front of our house. I wonder who did it.
   Information: **Sue** has a car, and she was out driving last night.
   Jane doesn't have a car, and she doesn't know how to drive.
   Don has a car, but I'm pretty sure he was at home last night.
   Ann was out driving last night, and today her car has a big dent in front.

   a. It couldn't have been _____.

   b. It must not have been _____.

   c. It could have been _____.

   d. It must have been _____.

3. *Situation:*   There is a very small hole in the bread. It looks like something ate some of the bread. The bread was in a closed drawer until I opened it.
   Information: **A mouse** likes to eat bread and is small enough to crawl into a drawer.
   A cat can't open a drawer.
   A rat can sometimes get into a drawer, but I'm pretty sure we don't have rats in our house.

   a. It could have been _____.

   b. It couldn't have been _____.

   c. It must have been _____.

4. *Situation:* My friends Mark and Carol are in the next room with my neighbor. I hear someone playing a very difficult song on the piano. I wonder who it is.

   Information: **Mark** has no musical ability at all and doesn't play any instrument.
   Carol is an excellent piano player.
   I don't think **my neighbor** plays the piano, but I'm not sure.

   a. It couldn't be _____.

   b. I suppose it could be _____.

   c. It must be _____.

5. *Situation:* The meeting starts in fifteen minutes. I wonder who is coming.

   Information: I just talked to **Bob** on the phone. He's on his way.
   Sally rarely misses a meeting.
   Janet is out of town.
   Andy comes to the meetings sometimes, and sometimes he doesn't.

   a. _____ won't be at the meeting.

   b. _____ should be at the meeting.

   c. _____ will be here.

   d. _____ might come.

6. *Situation:* I heard a loud crash in the next room. I rushed in immediately and found our antique vase on the floor. It was broken. I wondered what had happened.

   Information: Five-year-old **Bobby** was playing quietly with his toy truck.
   The cat was leaping frantically from table to table.
   The window was open, and **the breeze** was blowing gently through the room.

   a. _____ couldn't have knocked it off the table.

   b. _____ could have knocked it off the table, but it isn't likely.

   c. _____ must have knocked it off the table.

Directions: Complete the sentences with the appropriate form of the words in parentheses. Add *not* if necessary for a sentence to make sense.

1. A: Why wasn't Pamela at the meeting last night?

    B: She (*may + attend*) _____**may have been attending**_____ the lecture at Shaw Hall. I know she very much wanted to hear the speaker.

2. Alex has a test tomorrow that he needs to study for. He (*should + watch*) _____**shouldn't**_____ _____**be watching**_____ TV right now.

3. A: Why didn't Diane come to the phone? I know she was home when I called.

    B: I don't know. She (*might + wash*) _____ her hair when you called. Who knows?

4. There's Tom. He's standing at the bus stop. He (*must + wait*) _____ _____ for the 2 o'clock bus.

5. Kathy lost her way while driving to River City. She (*should + leave*) _____ _____ her road map at home.

6. A: Where's Ann?

    B: I don't know. She (*could + visit*) _____ her aunt and uncle right now. She usually visits them every Friday evening.

7. You (*should + watch*) _____ the movie on TV tonight. I highly recommend it. It's a classic.

8. I heard a loud crash in the next room. When I walked in, I found a brick on the floor, and the window was broken. Someone (*must + throw*) _____ the brick through the window.

9. Jack is in the employee lounge drinking coffee. He (*should + work*) _____ _____ on his report right now. It's due at 3:00 this afternoon. He (*should + waste*) _____ his time in the employee lounge.

10. A: Where's Jane? I haven't seen her for weeks.

    B: I'm not sure. She (*might + travel*) _____ in Europe. I think I heard her mention something about spending a few weeks in Europe this spring.

11. My tweed jacket isn't in my closet. I think my roommate (*might + borrow*) _____ _____ it. He often borrows my things without asking me.

12. Do you hear that guitar music? Carla (*must + play*) _____ her guitar.

13. A: When I arrived, Dennis looked surprised.

    B: He (*must + expect*) _____ you.

14. A: I couldn't reach Peter on the phone. I wonder where he was.

   B: He told me he was going to wash his car and then go to dinner at the Bistro Cafe. He
   (*might + wash*) _____ his car when you
   called, or he (*may + leave + already*) _____ for
   the restaurant by then.

◇ **PRACTICE 22—GUIDED STUDY: Forms of modals. (Charts 2-13 → 2-17)**

Directions: Complete the sentences with the appropriate form of the words in parentheses. Add *not*
if necessary for a sentence to make sense.

1. A: I need to see Tom. Where is he?

   B: In his room. Knock on his door softly. He (*might + take*) _____
   a nap.

2. When I walked into the room, the TV was on but the room was empty. Dad (*must + watch*)
   _____ TV a short while before I came into the
   room. He (*must + forget*) _____ to turn the TV off
   before he left the room.

3. Michael wanted to go to the opera, but he put off buying a ticket and now they're all sold. He
   (*should + buy*) _____ his ticket weeks ago. He (*should +
   wait*) _____ until now to try to get a ticket.

4. Bob was stopped by a police officer last night. He (*must + drive*) _____
   _____ too fast when she clocked him on her radar. She gave him a speeding
   ticket.

5. The staff (*must + plan*) _____ very well for the
   luncheon. There are still about ten people waiting to eat, and there's not enough food left.

6. A: Why didn't Jack answer the teacher when she asked him a question?

   B: He was too busy staring out the window. He (*must + daydream*) _____
   _____. He (*should + pay*)
   _____ attention. He (*should + stare*)
   _____ out the window during
   class yesterday.

7. A: Where's your bicycle?

   B: I don't know. One of my friends (*may + borrow*) _____
   it. Gee, I hope it wasn't stolen. Maybe Sally borrowed it.

   A: Sally? She (*could + borrow*) _____ it. She
   has a broken leg. Why would she want to borrow your bicycle?

8. George didn't do very well on the test because he didn't understand what he was supposed to
   do. He (*must + listen*) _____ very carefully when
   the teacher gave the directions.

9. A: Joan was really upset when she found out that someone had told Alan about the surprise birthday party she gave him last night. She thinks Joe told him.

   B: Joe (*could + tell*) _____ him about it. He was out of town until just before the party. He barely got there in time from the airport.

10. A: Art has two full-time jobs this summer to make some money for school in the fall. He (*must + have*) _____ very much time to rest and do other things.

    B: That might explain why no one answered the door when I stopped by his house a little while ago. He (*must + sleep*) _____.

11. A: Kathy just bought a new car, and now she's looking for a new apartment.

    B: She (*must + make*) _____ a lot of money in her new job.

12. A: Where's that cold air coming from?

    B: Someone (*must + leave*) _____ the door open.

13. A: The roads are treacherous this morning. In places, they're nothing but a sheet of ice. I (*should + take*) _____ the bus to work this morning instead of driving my car. I thought I'd never make it!

    B: I know. It's terrible outside. Jake still hasn't arrived. He (*must + walk*) _____ _____ to work right now. He doesn't live too far away, and I know he hates to drive on icy roads.

    A: He (*might + decide*) _____ not to come in at all. He (*could + work*) _____ on his report at home this morning. I'll check with his secretary. He (*may + call*) _____ her by now.

◇ PRACTICE 23—GUIDED STUDY: Degrees of certainty. (Charts 2-13 → 2-17)

Directions: Go to a public place, a place where there are people whom you do not know (a cafeteria, store, street corner, park, zoo, lobby, etc.). Choose three of these people to write a composition about. Using a paragraph for each person, describe his/her appearance briefly and then make "guesses" about this person: age, occupation, personality, activities, etc.

Example: I'm in a hotel lobby. I'm looking at a man who is wearing a blue pin-striped suit and carrying a briefcase. He is talking to someone at the registration desk, so he must be registering to stay in the hotel. He couldn't be checking out, because people have to check out at a different desk. He might be simply asking a question, but I doubt it. Judging from his clothes, I'd say he's probably a businessman. But he could be something else. He might be a doctor, or a funeral director, or a professor. He has salt-and-pepper hair and not too many wrinkles. He must be about 50 or 55. He doesn't have any luggage with him. The porter must have taken his luggage. The hotel clerk just handed the man a key. Aha! I was right. He is registering to stay at the hotel.

◇ PRACTICE 24—SELFSTUDY: *Used to* and *be used to*. (Chart 2-18)

Directions: Complete the sentences with *used to* or *be used to* and the correct form of the verbs in parentheses.

1. I (*live*) __*used to live*__ in Jakarta, but now I live in Paris.

2. I (*live*) __*am used to living*__ in Jakarta. I've lived here all my life.

3. Jane (*work*) _____ for the telephone company, but now she has a job at the post office.

4. This work doesn't bother me. I (*work*) _____ hard. I've worked hard all my life.

5. Dick (*have*) _____ a mustache, but he doesn't anymore. He shaved it off because his wife didn't like it. I (*see, not*) _____ him without his mustache. He still looks strange to me.

6. When I was a child, I (*think*) _____ anyone over 40 was old. Of course, now that I'm middle-aged, I agree with those who say, "Life begins at 40."

7. It (*take*) _____ weeks or months to cross the Atlantic Ocean from Europe to the Americas, but now it takes only a matter of hours.

8. Even though Jason is only 12, he (*fly*) _____ on airplanes. His father is a pilot and has taken Jason with him in a plane many times.

9. When I was growing up, my mother often sent me to the neighborhood store to get something for her. And each time I went there, Mr. Ditmar, the owner, (*give*) _____ me a piece of candy.

10. Michael (*take*) _____ care of himself. He left home when he was 15 and has been on his own ever since.

◇ PRACTICE 25—GUIDED STUDY: *Used to* and *be used to*. (Chart 2-18)

Directions: Complete the sentences with *used to* or *be used to* and the correct form of the verbs in parentheses.

1. I (*play*) _____ the piano quite well when I was younger. Now, I'm not sure I could play anything if I tried. It's been too many years.

2. I (*drive*) _____ on busy highways in big cities. I've been doing it ever since I learned how to drive.

3. The early pioneers in the United States (*rely*) _____ heavily on hunting and fishing for their food.

4. My feet are killing me! I (*stand, not*) _____ for long periods of time. Let's find a place to sit down.

5. I (*come*) _____ to work ten minutes early. I hoped that my boss would notice and give me a raise in pay. It didn't work, so I stopped coming early.

6. People (*think*) _____ the world was flat.

7. I never (*like*) _____ opera, but after seeing *Madame Butterfly* last night, I've changed my mind. I thoroughly enjoyed it.

8. I (*take*) _____ a shower every morning before I go to work. I rarely miss a morning.

9. Marge and Fred (*commute*) _____ into the city to work every day. They've been doing it for two years and don't seem to mind the one-hour drive each way.

10. I (*travel*) _____ nearly two weeks out of every month, but now I do most of my work at the home office and seldom have to go out of town.

◇ **PRACTICE 26—SELFSTUDY: Repeated action: *would*. (Chart 2-19)**

Directions: Complete the sentences using ***would*** and the verbs in the list. Use each verb only one time. Include any words in parentheses.

bring	drive	listen	throw
call	fall	take	wipe
✔ come	knock	tell	✔ yell

1. My father never liked to talk on the phone. Whenever it rang, he (*always*) __***would***__ __***always yell***__, "I'm not here!" Usually, he was only joking and __***would***__ __***come***__ to the phone when it was for him.

2. I'll always remember Miss Emerson, my fifth grade teacher. Sometimes a student _____ asleep in her class. Whenever that happened, Miss Emerson _____ a piece of chalk at the student!

3. Until we finally had a long talk about it, my Aunt Pat (*never*) _____ before coming over. In fact, she (*not even*) _____ on the door. She would just walk right in and catch us all by surprise.

4. I have fond childhood memories of my Uncle Joe. Whenever he came to visit, he (*always*) _____ me a little present.

5. When our kids were still living at home, I liked to go out to eat with my family. On every pay day, I _____ the family to some restaurant for dinner.

6. People acquire strange habits. For example, my Uncle Oscar, who lived with us when I was a child, (*always*) _____ his plate with his napkin whenever he sat down to a meal.

7. I'll never forget evenings spent with my grandparents when I was a child. My grandmother _____ stories of her childhood seventy years ago, and we _____ intently and question her for every detail.

8. When I was a salesman, it seemed to me that I was in my car most of the time. I _____ to work to pick up my schedule, and then go from place to place all day, calling on small businesses.

Directions: Complete the sentences with your own words.

1. I went to an opera last night. I would rather _____ **have gone to a movie** _____.

2. I wrecked my father's car. I'd rather not ____ **face him** ____, but I have to.

3. Bobby said he'd rather _____
   for his birthday than _____.

4. Sometimes teenagers would rather _____

5. I studied French when I was in high school only because my parents wanted me to. I would
   rather _____

6. I know you want to know, but I'd rather not _____.
   I told Marge that I'd keep it a secret.

7. I would rather _____ right after dinner at the restaurant last night,
   but my friends insisted on going back to John's apartment to listen to some music and talk.
   Tonight, I'd really rather not _____. I want to get a good night's sleep
   for the first time all week.

8. I'd rather _____ than _____
   when we go camping.

9. A: Would you rather _____ or _____
      tonight?

   B: Actually, I'd rather _____. My favorite show is on tonight.

10. I would rather _____ last night than
    _____, but _____.

Directions: Complete the sentences with *could* and the verb in parentheses *if possible.* If the use of
could is not possible, provide any other appropriate completion.

1. When I was younger, I ____ **could stay** ____ up late without getting sleepy, but now I always go to
   bed early. (*stay*)

2. Last night we ____ **went** ____ to a restaurant. The food was delicious. (*go*)

3. The teacher gave the students plenty of time for the test yesterday. All of them _____
   _____ it before the time was up. (*complete*)

4. I was tired, but I _____ my work before I went to bed last night. (*finish*)

5. Last night I _____ TV for a couple of hours. Then I studied. (*watch*)

6. I like to ride my bicycle. I _____ it to work when we lived on First Street,
   but now I can't. Now I have to drive because we live too far away. (*ride*)

7. Susan _____ her bicycle to work yesterday instead of walking. (*ride*)

8. The picnic yesterday was a lot of fun. All of us _____ it a lot. (*enjoy*)

9. After years of devoted work, Mr. Bailey finally _____ a raise in salary last April. (*get*)

10. I (*swim*) _____ long distances when I was a teenager.

11. I had to put together my daughter's tricycle. It came from the factory unassembled. It was a struggle and took me a long time, but in the end I _____ it together. (*get*)

◇ **PRACTICE 29—GUIDED STUDY: Modals: dialogues. (Chapter 2)**

Directions: Complete the following dialogues with your own words. Add necessary punctuation.

1. A: Why don't we *go to Luigi's Restaurant for lunch?* _____

   B: Thanks, but I can't. I have to *stay and finish this report over lunchtime.* _____

   A: That's too bad.

   B: I should have *come to work early this morning to finish it,* _____ but

   I couldn't. I had to drop my daughter off at school _____

   and meet with her teacher. _____

2. A: I _____

   B: You shouldn't have done that!

   A: I know, but _____

   B: Well, why don't _____

3. A: _____

    B: No, he had to _____

    A: Why?

    B: _____

4. A: Did you hear the news? We don't have to _____

    B: Why not?

    A: _____

    B: Well, then, why don't _____

5. A: Whose _____

    B: I don't know. It _____ or it _____

    A: Can _____

    B: I'll try.

6. A: _____

    B: Not at all. I'd be happy to.

    A: Thank you. Maybe sometime _____

7. A: _____

    B: I would have liked to, but I _____

8. A: You must not _____

    B: Why not?

    A: _____

9. A: _____

    B: Well, you'd better _____ or _____

    A: I know, but _____

10. A: _____

    B: _____ but I'd rather not have gone.

       I'd rather _____

11. A: May I _____

    B: Please do. I _____

    A: We could, but it's going to _____

12. A: _____

    B: That can't be true! She couldn't have _____

    A: Oh? Why not? Why do you say that?

    B: Because _____

Directions: Work in pairs. Using the given situations, create dialogues of 10 to 20 sentences or more. Then present your dialogues to the rest of the class. For each situation, the beginning of the dialogue is given. Try to include appropriate modals in your conversation.

1. *Situation:*   *The two of you are roommates or a married couple. It is late at night. All of the lights are turned off. You hear a strange noise. You try to figure out what it might or must be, what you should or should not do, etc.*

   Dialogue: A: Psst. Are you awake?
   B: Yes. What's the matter?
   A: Do you hear that noise?
   B: Yes, what do you suppose it is?
   A: I don't know. It . . . .
   B: . . . .

2. *Situation:*   *Your teacher is always on time, but today it is fifteen minutes past the time class begins and he/she still isn't here. You try to figure out why he/she isn't here yet and what you should do.*

   Dialogue: A: Mr./Mrs./Ms./Miss/Dr./Professor _____ should have been here fifteen minutes ago. I wonder where s/he is. Why do you suppose s/he hasn't arrived yet?
   B: Well, ...

3. *Situation:*   *The two of you are planning to go on a picnic. You are almost ready to leave when you hear a loud noise. It sounds like thunder. You are supposed to meet Nancy and Paul at the park for your picnic.*

   Dialogue: A: Is the picnic basket all packed?
   B: Yes. Everything is ready to go.
   A: Good. Let's get going.
   B: Wait. Did you hear that?
   A: . . . .

4. *Situation:*   *It is late at night. The weather is very bad. Your eighteen-year-old son, who had gone to a party with some of his friends, was supposed to be home an hour ago. (The two of you are either a married couple or a parent and his/her friend.) You are getting worried. You are trying to figure out where he might be, what might or must have happened, and what you should do, if anything.*

   Dialogue: A: It's already _____ o'clock and _____ isn't home yet. I'm getting worried.
   B: So am I. Where do you suppose he is?
   A: . . . .

◇ **PRACTICE 31—GUIDED STUDY:** Discussion using modals. (Chapter 2)

Directions: In small discussion groups, debate one, some, or all of the following statements. At the end of the discussion time, choose one member of your group to summarize for the rest of the class the principal ideas during the discussion.

Do you agree with the following statements? Why or why not?

1. Violence on television influences people to act violently.
2. Cigarette smoking should be banned from all public places.
3. No family should have more than two children.
4. Books, films, and news should be censored by government agencies.
5. People shouldn't marry until they are at least twenty-five years old.
6. All nuclear weapons in the possession of any nation should be eliminated.
7. The United Nations is a productive and essential organization.
8. All people of the world should speak the same language.

◇ **PRACTICE 32—GUIDED STUDY:** General review of verb forms. (Chapters 1 and 2)

Directions: Complete the sentences with the words in parentheses. Use any appropriate tense or modal.

A: Yesterday I (*1. have*) _____ a bad day.

B: Oh? What (*2. happen*) _____?

A: I was supposed to be at a job interview at ten, but I didn't make it because while I (*3. drive*) _____ down the freeway, my car (*4. break*) _____ down.

B: What (*5. do, you*) _____?

A: I (*6. pull*) _____ over to the side of the road, (*7. get*) _____ out, and (*8. start*) _____ walking.

B: You (*9. do, not*) _____ that. Walking alone along a highway can be dangerous. You (*10. stay*) _____ in your car until help came.

A: You (*11. be, probably*) _____ right, but I (*12. start*) _____ walking down the highway. After I (*13. walk*) _____ for about 20 minutes, I got to an exit ramp. Near the bottom of the exit ramp, there was a restaurant with a public phone. I (*14. go*) _____ to the phone and (*15. discover*) _____ that I had left my purse in the car, so I (*16. have, not*) _____ any money to make a phone call.

B: What did you do then?

A: What do you think I should have done?

B: I don't know. I (*17. think*) _____ of several things. You (*18. go*) _____ _____ back to your car for your purse. You (*19. try*) _____ _____ to borrow some change from a customer in the restaurant. You

(20. *ask*) _____ to use the private phone in the restaurant. What did you actually do?

A: I (21. *ask*) _____ to speak with the manager of the restaurant.

B: That was a good idea. That's exactly what you should have done. What did the manager do?

A: When I (22. *tell*) _____ her my tale of woe, she (23. *be*) _____ very sympathetic. She (24. *allow*) _____ me to use her private phone to call my friend Bill, who (25. *drive*) _____ to the restaurant.

B: You (26. *feel*) _____ really glad when you saw Bill.

A: I did. First he (27. *take*) _____ me to my job interview, and then he (28. *take*) _____ care of the car.

B: Good friends are important, aren't they?

A: They sure are.

B: Did you get the job you interviewed for?

A: I don't know yet. I (29. *get*) _____ it, or I might not. I just don't know. I (30. *know*) _____ in a couple more days.

B: Good luck!

A: Thanks! I need it! Well, I (31. *leave*) _____ now. I (32. *be*) _____ _____ at a meeting in 45 minutes. (33. *I, use*) _____ _____ your phone? I (34. *need*) _____ to call a taxi. My car is still in the garage, and I (35. *have, not*) _____ time to wait for a bus.

B: I (36. *take*) _____ you to your meeting.

A: Really? Thanks. As you said, good friends are important!

◇ PRACTICE 33—GUIDED STUDY: Review of modals. (Chapter 2)

Directions: Choose three of the following topics. Write a short paragraph on each.

1. Write about when, where, and why you should (or should not) have done something in your life.
2. Write about a time in your life when you did something you did not want to do. Why did you do it? What could you have done differently? What should you have done? What would you rather have done?
3. Look at your future. What will, might, should it be like? Write about what you should, must, can do now in order to make your life what you want it to be.
4. Write about one embarrassing incident in your life. What could, should, might you have done to avoid it?
5. Look at the world situation in relationships between nations. What could, should (or should not), must (or must not) be done to improve understanding?
6. Choose one of the environmental problems people are considering today. What could, should, may, must, might be done to solve this problem?

Directions: Choose the correct completion.

Example:

___C___ Peter _____ *rather sleep on a mattress than on the floor.*
      A. shall   *B. could*   *C. would*   *D. must*

___B___ 1. Al painted his bedroom black. It looks dark and dreary. He _____ a different color.
    A. had to choose   B. should have chosen
    C. must have chosen   D. could have been choosing

___D___ 2. Tom is sitting at his desk. He's reading his chemistry text because he has a test tomorrow. He _____.
    A. could study   B. should be studying
    C. will study   D. must be studying

D   ___A___ 3. When Mr. Lee was younger, he _____ work in the garden for hours, but now he has to take frequent rests because he has emphysema.
    A. has got to   B. can
    C. should be able to   D. could

A   ___D___ 4. Whenever my parents went out in the evening, I _____ the job of taking care of my younger brother.
    A. would get   B. should get
    C. must have gotten   D. had better get

B   ___A___ 5. Yesterday I _____ to a furniture store. I bought a new lamp there.
    A. could go   B. went
    C. could have gone   D. ought to have gone

___B___ 6. Jimmy and Maria were mischievous children. They _____ tricks on their teachers, which always got them into a lot of trouble.
    A. could play   B. used to play
    C. could have played   D. may have played

D   ___A___ 7. Robert has a new car. He _____ it for a very good price. He paid 30 percent less than the regular retail cost.
    A. could buy   B. had to buy
    C. was supposed to buy   D. was able to buy

___C___ 8. "Did you enjoy the picnic?"
    "It was okay, but I'd rather _____ to a movie."
    A. go   B. be going   C. have gone   D. went

___D___ 9. "Why are you so sure that Ann didn't commit the crime she's been accused of committing?"
    "She _____ that crime because I was with her, and we were out of town on that day."
    A. may not have committed   B. wasn't supposed to commit
    C. committed   D. couldn't have committed.

A   ___B___ 10. "Since we have to be there in a hurry, we _____ take a taxi."
    "I agree."
    A. had better   B. may
    C. have been used to   D. are able to

D   ___C___ 11. "It _____ rain this evening. Why don't you take an umbrella?"
    "That's a good idea. May I borrow yours?"
    A. had better   B. could be   C. must   D. might

Chapter 2

12. "_____ you hand me that pair of scissors, please?"
"Certainly."
    A. May   B. Shall   C. Will   D. Should

13. "Larry drove all night to get here for his sister's wedding. He _____ exhausted by the time he arrived."
"He was."
    A. ought to be   B. could be
    C. must have been   D. will have been

14. "What are you doing here now? You _____ be here for another three hours."
"I know. We got an early start and it took less time than we expected. I hope you don't mind."
    A. couldn't   B. might not
    C. had better not   D. aren't supposed to

15. "_____ taking me downtown on your way to work this morning?"
"Not at all."
    A. Can you   B. Why don't you
    C. Would you mind   D. Could you please

16. "I locked myself out of my apartment. I didn't know what to do."
"You _____ your roommate."
    A. could have called   B. may have called
    C. would have called   D. must have called

17. "You haven't eaten anything since yesterday afternoon. You _____ be really hungry!"
"I am."
    A. might   B. will   C. can   D. must

18. "How long have you been married?"
"We _____ have been married for twenty-three years on our next anniversary."
    A. must   B. should   C. will   D. could

19. "I _____ there at 6 P.M. for the meeting, but my car won't start. Could you please give me a lift in your car?"
"Sure. Are you ready to go now?"
    A. will be   B. may be
    C. supposed to be   D. have got to be

20. "I left a cookie on the table, but now it's gone. What happened to it?"
"I don't know. One of the children _____ it."
    A. may have eaten   B. could eat
    C. had to eat   D. should have eaten

◇ PRACTICE TEST B—GUIDED STUDY: Modals and similar expressions. (Chapter 2)

Directions: Choose the correct completion.

Example:

__C__ *Peter _____ rather sleep on a mattress than on the floor.*
    A. shall   *B. could*   *C. would*   *D. must*

1. "My boss is always looking over my shoulder whenever I do anything."
"That _____ bother you."
"But it does."
    A. shouldn't   B. might not   C. may not   D. won't

_____ 2. "This movie is boring and too violent."
"I agree. _____ leave?"
    A. Will we   B. Why don't we   C. Must we   D. Would we

_____ 3. "Chris, you _____ the fish in the refrigerator before it spoils."
"You're right. I didn't know it was still in the shopping bag."
    A. had better put   B. had to put
    C. would rather put   D. may put

_____ 4. "What does Mr. Griffin do for a living?"
"Nothing. He's very rich. He _____ work for a living."
    A. must not   B. shouldn't
    C. doesn't have to   D. hadn't better

_____ 5. "Why are you so late?"
"I _____ my aunt to the airport. The traffic was terrible!"
    A. could take   B. must have taken
    C. should take   D. had to take

_____ 6. "I heard that Laura was offered a job at a top computer firm in Chicago."
"Oh? That's wonderful! She _____ very pleased."
    A. is supposed to be   B. might be
    C. must be   D. is

_____ 7. "The hot weather doesn't seem to bother you."
"When I had my farm, I _____ work in the hot fields for hours."
    A. used to   B. ought to   C. must   D. had better

_____ 8. "They towed my car away from the executive parking lot yesterday."
"You _____ have parked there."
    A. may not   B. should not   C. must not   D. might not

_____ 9. "Are you going to have a big birthday party for your father?"
"Not this year, but next year. He _____ 50 years old then."
    A. should be   B. must be   C. will be   D. has to be

_____ 10. "I need some help with this table. _____ you lift the other end, please?"
"Sure, just a second."
    A. May   B. Should   C. Could   D. Shall

_____ 11. "How did you get my telephone number? It's not listed in the phone book, so you _____ have found it in the directory."
"I got it from your mother."
    A. may not   B. won't   C. might not   D. couldn't

_____ 12. "Is that volcano dormant or active?"
"Active. According to the experts, it _____ erupt again in the very near future."
    A. would   B. may be   C. could   D. had better

_____ 13. "Last year I _____ this fine print in these contracts, but now I can't."
"You'd better go to the eye doctor."
    A. could read   B. must have read
    C. should have read   D. had to read

_____ 14. "Is littering against the law?"
"Yes. There's a law that says that you _____ throw trash on the streets."
    A. don't have to   B. must not   C. couldn't   D. might not

_____ 15. "Do you want to go to the seashore for vacation?"
"I think I'd rather _____ to the mountains."
    A. to go   B. going   C. go   D. have gone

_____ 16. "Barbara just told me that she can't go to the meeting tonight."
"She _____ go! We need her there for the financial report."
    A. has got to   B. has gotten to   C. have to   D. must be

_____ 17. "_____ letting me use your bicycle for a little while?"
"Not at all."
    A. Please to   B. Would you mind
    C. Will you   D. Could you please

_____ 18. "We _____ be here. That sign says 'No Trespassing.'"
"It's too late now. We're already here."
    A. couldn't   B. don't have to
    C. might not   D. aren't supposed to

_____ 19. "Harry's new jacket doesn't seem to fit him very well."
"He _____ it on before he bought it."
    A. must have tried   B. was able to try
    C. should have tried   D. may have tried

_____ 20. "Do you like to play tennis?"
"Yes. When I worked at the embassy, I _____ meet a friend at 5 every afternoon for a game."
    A. would   B. should   C. had better   D. would rather

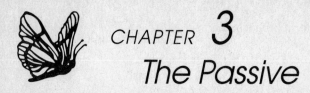

CHAPTER 3
The Passive

◇ **PRACTICE 1—SELFSTUDY: Forming the passive. (Chart 3-1)**

Directions: Change the active to the passive by writing the correct form of *be* in the blanks. Use the same tense for *be* in the passive sentence that is used in the active sentence.

Example:
Mrs. Bell answered my question. . . . . *My question* __**was**__ **answered** by Mrs. Bell.

1. *simple present:*
   Authors write books. . . . . Books _____ **written** by authors.
2. *present progressive:*
   Mr. Brown is writing that book. . . . . That book _____ **written** by Mr. Brown.
3. *present perfect:*
   Ms. Lee has written the report. . . . . The report _____ **written** by Ms. Lee.
4. *simple past:*
   Bob wrote that letter. That letter _____ **written** by Bob.
5. *past progressive:*
   A student was writing the report. . . . . The report _____ **written** by a student.
6. *past perfect:*
   Lucy had written a memo. . . . . A memo _____ **written** by Lucy.
7. *simple future:*
   Your teacher will write a report. . . . . A report _____ **written** by your teacher.
8. *be going to:*
   Tom is going to write the letter. . . . . The letter _____ **written** by Tom.
9. *future perfect:*
   Alice will have written the report. . . . . The report _____ **written** by Alice.

10. The judges have made a decision. . . . . A decision _____ **made** by the judges.

11. Several people saw the accident. . . . . The accident _____ **seen** by several people.

12. Ann is sending the letters. . . . . The letters _____ **sent** by Ann.

13. Fred will plan the party. . . . . The party _____ **planned** by Fred.

14. The medicine had cured my illness. . . . . My illness _____ **cured** by the medicine.

15. The cat will have caught the mouse. . . . . . . The mouse _____ **caught** by the cat.

16. Engineers design bridges. . . . . Bridges _____ **designed** by engineers.

17. The city is going to build a bridge. . . . . A bridge _____ **built** by the city.

18. A guard was protecting the jewels. . . . . The jewels _____ **protected** by a guard.

Directions: Change the following sentences to the passive.

1. a. QUESTION: Did Tom write that report? → *Was that report written by Tom?*
   b. NEGATIVE: No, he didn't write it. → *No, it wasn't written by him.*
   c. AFFIRMATIVE: Alice wrote it. → *It was written by Alice.*

2. a. QUESTION: Is Mr. Brown painting your house?
   b. NEGATIVE: No, he isn't painting it.
   c. AFFIRMATIVE: My uncle is painting it.

3. a. QUESTION: Will Steve wash the dishes?
   b. NEGATIVE: No, he won't wash them.
   c. AFFIRMATIVE: The children will wash them.

4. a. Has Sue planned the meeting?
   b. No, she hasn't planned it.
   c. The committee has planned it.

5. a. Does Mr. Parr play that violin?
   b. No, he doesn't play it.
   c. His son plays it.

6. a. Is Jack going to return the books to the library?
   b. No, he isn't going to return them.
   c. His sister is going to return them.

7. a. Did the archeologists discover the ancient skeleton?
   b. No, they didn't discover it.
   c. A farmer discovered it.

8. a. Was Sally preparing the food?
   b. No, she wasn't preparing it.
   c. Her mother was preparing it.

9. a. Will Ms. Anderson have typed the letters?
   b. No, she won't have typed them.
   c. The secretary will have typed them.

◇ PRACTICE 3—SELFSTUDY: Forming the passive. (Chart 3-1 and Appendix 1, Units B and C)

Directions: In the following, active sentences are changed to passive sentences. Complete the passive sentence with the appropriate verb form. Keep the same tense. Use question and negative forms as necessary.

1. Did Ann discover the mistake?

   → ___**Was**___ the mistake ___**discovered**___ by Ann?

2. A famous author wrote that book.

   → That book ___**was written**___ by a famous author.

3. Jack won't pay the bill.

   → The bill ___**won't be paid**___ by Jack.

4. The waiter refilled my glass.

   → My glass _____ by the waiter.

5. Did Sue knock that vase to the floor?

   → _____ that vase _____ to the floor by Sue?

6. Tommy didn't break the chair.

   → The chair _____ by Tommy.

7. Alan's knowledge about art doesn't impress me.

   → I _____ by Alan's knowledge about art.

8. One of the parents is taping the children's song.

   → The children's song _____ by one of the parents.

9. Is a student pilot flying that airplane?

   → _____ that airplane _____ by a student pilot?

10. The best chess player will win the match.

   → The match _____ by the best chess player.

11. Your emotional appeals will not influence the judge.

   → The judge _____ by your emotional appeals.

12. The voters are going to decide that issue.

   → That issue _____ by the voters.

13. The city attorney has discovered new evidence.

   → New evidence _____ by the city attorney.

14. Mr. Snow hasn't taught that course since 1985.

   → That course _____ by Mr. Snow since 1985.

15. Had a special messenger delivered the package before you got to the office?

   → _____ the package _____ by a special messenger
   before you got to the office?

16. The pollution in the city was affecting Tim's breathing.

   → Tim's breathing _____ by the pollution in the city.

Directions: In the following sentences, some of the verbs are transitive and some are intransitive. Identify the verb of the sentence. Then identify the object of the verb if there is one. If the verb has an object, change the sentence to the passive. Use the symbol Ø to indicate "none."

	VERB	OBJECT OF VERB	PASSIVE SENTENCE
1. Al will pay the bill.	will pay	the bill	The bill will be paid by Al.
2. Sue will come tomorrow.	will come	ø	ø
3. The hotel supplies towels.			
4. Accidents happen every day.			
5. Everyone noticed my mistake.			
6. The train arrived at three.			
7. The news didn't surprise me.			
8. Did the news surprise you?			
9. The sun wasn't shining.			
10. Ann interrupted my story.			
11. Do ghosts exist?			
12. Birds fly in the sky.			
13. Will Ed come tomorrow?			
14. Mr. Lee died last year.			
15. Did Bob throw the ball?			
16. Sue laughed loudly.			
17. An old man told the story.			
18. It hasn't rained lately.			

◇ PRACTICE 5—SELFSTUDY: Forming the passive. (Chart 3-1)

Directions: Change the following active sentences to passive if possible. Some of the verbs are intransitive and cannot be changed. Keep the same tense.

1. My uncle will meet you at the airport. → *You will be met at the airport by my uncle.*

2. Our plane will land at 6:03. → *(no change)*

3. The chef will prepare the food.

4. John is working at the bakery.

5. Lightning didn't cause the fire.

6. We walked downtown after work yesterday.

7. Thousands of people ride the subway every day.

8. The baby was crying in his crib.

9. I don't agree with you.

10. Joe fell down on his way to school this morning.

11. George seemed unhappy yesterday.

12. A special committee is going to settle the dispute.

13. Our houseguests are going to arrive sometime tomorrow afternoon.

14. Our plan succeeded at last.

15. Barbara traveled to Uganda last year.

16. Did the army surround the enemy?

17. What happened in class yesterday?

18. The Persians invented windmills around 1500 years ago.

◇ PRACTICE 6—SELFSTUDY: Active vs. passive. (Chart 3-1)

Directions: Complete the sentences with the words in parentheses. Some of the sentences are active and some are passive. Use any appropriate tense.

1. You (notify) __*will be notified*__ by my secretary next week.

2. Last night I (remember, not) __*didn't remember*__ to lock my front door.

3. At the present time, the oldest house in town (restore) _____

   by the Historical Society. When the restoration is finished, the house is sure to be a popular

   tourist attraction.

4. A: What a beautiful old wooden chest!

   B: It (build) _____ by my grandfather over fifty years ago.

5. At one time, the entire world (*rule*) _____ by dinosaurs. Some dinosaurs (*walk*) _____ on their hind legs and (*stand*) _____ as tall as palm trees.

6. Disneyland is a world famous amusement park in Southern California. It (*visit*) _____ _____ by more than ten million people every year.

7. Many of us take water for granted in our daily lives, but people who live in the desert (*use, not*) _____ water carelessly. To them, each drop is precious.

8. I (*agree, not*) _____ with people who say space exploration is a waste of money. What do you think?

9. Do you really think that we (*invade*) _____ by creatures from outer space in the near future?

10. Most insects (*live*) _____ for less than a year. The common housefly (*live*) _____ from 19 to 30 days.

11. (*You, accept, already*) _____ by this university when you heard about the other scholarship?

12. I got into a taxi quickly because I (*follow*) _____ by two strange men. As soon as I got into the taxi, I (*feel*) _____ a little safer.

13. The impact of the earthquake yesterday (*feel*) _____ by people who lived hundreds of kilometers from the epicenter.

14. When Alex was only ten, his father (*die*) _____.

15. Mark (*influence*) _____ a lot by his friends, isn't he? He should be more independent and think for himself.

16. A few days ago, my car (*steal*) _____ by one of the teenagers in my neighborhood. He (*catch*) _____ by the police a few blocks from my house. He just wanted to take it for a drive, but now he's in a lot of trouble.

◇ PRACTICE 7—SELFSTUDY: Using the "*by* phrase." (Chart 3-2)

Directions: Change the active sentences to passive. Keep the same tense. Include the "*by phrase*" only if necessary.

1. People grow rice in India. → *Rice is grown in India.*   (*no "by phrase"*)

2. My aunt made this rug. → *This rug was made by my aunt.*

3. They are fixing my car today. → *My car is being fixed today.*   (*no "by phrase"*)

4. They speak French in Quebec.

5. Mr. Eads designed that bridge in the 1870s.

6. Someone invented the wheel thousands of years ago.

7. Did Thomas Edison invent the telephone?

8. They are going to build a new hospital just outside of town.

9. How do people make candles?

10. Very few people watch that TV show.

11. Look! Someone is feeding the seals.

◇ **PRACTICE 8—GUIDED STUDY: Using the "*by* phrase." (Chart 3-2)**

Directions: Change the active sentences to passive. Keep the same tense. Include the "***by*** *phrase*" only if necessary.

1. Someone cut down that tree last week. → *That tree was cut down last week.*   *(no "**by**" phrase)*

2. Sally made that pie. → *That pie was made by Sally.*

3. Someone is considering Jack for that job.

4. Three continents surround the Mediterranean Sea.

5. I got upset when someone interrupted me in the middle of my story.

6. When Robert returned home, each of his relatives embraced him.

7. People didn't build Rome in a day.

8. Where do they file that information?

9. Before we arrived, someone had chained the dog to the fence in the backyard.

10. Did the noise from the neighbor's apartment annoy you last night?

11. As soon as it happened, people broadcast the news all over the world.

12. Do they make those tractors in this country, or do they import them?

13. While I was walking down the street, a nice young man in a military uniform approached me.

14. They will not provide pencils at the test, so please bring your own.

◇ **PRACTICE 9—SELFSTUDY:** Indirect objects as passive subjects. (Chart 3-3)

Directions: Identify the indirect object (**I.O.**). Change the sentences to the passive by using the *indirect object* as the subject of the sentence. Use the "*by phrase*" only if necessary. Keep the same tense.

                                          I.O.

1. Someone is going to serve Jack breakfast in bed on his birthday.

   → *Jack is going to be served breakfast in bed on his birthday.*

2. Someone has offered Mike the opportunity to study abroad.

3. People don't pay babysitters a lot of money.

4. When I was living in Kuwait, my neighbor taught me Arabic.

5. Someone awarded Jason a medal for distinguished service in the military.

6. The real estate office will send you a copy of the sales contract.

7. Someone handed me a telegram when I answered the door.

8. The director of the museum, Ms. Cynthia Hall, is going to give the schoolchildren a special tour of the modern art exhibit.

9. People gave Mr. French a gold watch upon his retirement from the company.

◇ **PRACTICE 10—SELFSTUDY:** Active and passive. (Charts 3-1 → 3-3)

Directions: Complete the sentences with the given words. Some of the sentences are passive and some are active. Use any appropriate tense.

1. The examination papers are scored by machine. The students (*tell*) ___*will be told*___ their results next week.

2. The project got finished early. The committee (*complete*) ___*completed*___ its work three weeks ahead of schedule.

3. The teacher (*assist*) _____ by two graduate students during the exam yesterday.

4. During the family celebration, the little boy was crying because he (*ignore*) _____ _____. He needed some attention, too.

5. A: Where (*buy, you*) _____ that beautiful necklace?

   B: I (*buy, not*) _____ it. It (*give*) _____ to me for my birthday. (*like, you*) _____ it?

6. Soon after I (*apply*) _____ for a job with the United Nations two years ago, I (*hire*) _____.

7. The crocodiles at the zoo look like statues. They (*lie*) _____ perfectly still for hours at a time. They have no need to move because they don't have to hunt for their food. They (*feed*) _____ regularly by the zookeepers.

8. This lovely beach won't exist forever. Eventually, it (*erode, probably*) _____ _____ away by the sea, and there will be nothing left but bedrock. The geologic forces of nature never stop.

9. Yesterday we went to look at an apartment. I really liked it, but by the time we got there, it (*rent, already*) _____.

10. Bananas originated in Asia. They (*introduce*) _____ to the Americas in 1516. Until the 1860s, bananas (*eat*) _____ principally by people of the tropics. Today, bananas (*export*) _____ to all parts of the world, and they (*enjoy*) _____ by people who live in all climates.

11. There's going to be a story in the local newspaper about my neighbor, Mrs. Morris. Tomorrow she (*interview*) _____ by one of the local reporters about her doll collection. Over the years, she (*collect*) _____ more than 400 dolls from all over the world.

12. The sun is just one of billions of stars in the universe. As it travels through space, it (*circle*) _____ by many other celestial bodies. The nine known planets (*hold*) _____ in orbit by the sun's gravitational field. The planets, in turn, (*circle*) _____ by their own satellites, or moons.

13. Early inhabitants of this region (*worship*) _____ the sun and the moon. We know this from the jewelry, sculptures, and other art work archaeologists have found.

◇ PRACTICE 11—GUIDED STUDY: Active and passive. (Charts 3-1 → 3-3)

Directions: Complete the sentences with the given words. Some of the sentences are passive and some are active. Use any appropriate tense.

1. Ali and Mustafa (*complain*) _____ to the landlord many times since they moved into their present apartment, but to date nothing (*do*) _____ about the leak in the roof and the broken window in the bedroom.

2. Yesterday I told my teenage daughter to clean her room before she (*go*) _____ to school. After she had left the house, I looked in her room. She (*pile*) _____ all of her clothes on a chair. Everything else (*shove*) _____ under the bed.

3. Sometimes people (*intimidate*) _____ by salespeople. As a result, sometimes they (*buy*) _____ things that they don't really want.

4. Two days ago I (*put*) _____ an ad in the classified section of the newspaper so I could find a buyer for my old car. Yesterday I (*sell*) _____ it. It (*buy*) _____ by a teenager who (*look*) _____ for an old car to fix up himself. Today a friend of mine told me that he wanted to buy my old car, but he was too late. By the time he talked to me, the car (*sell, already*) _____ to the teenager.

5. The wheel (*invent*) _____ over 5,000 years ago. Throughout history, it (*assist*) _____ people in making better use of oxen, horses, and other animals in transporting goods.

6. Captain Cook, a British navigator, was the first European to reach Australia's east coast. While his ship was lying off Australia, his sailors (*bring*) _____ a strange animal on board. Cook wanted to know the name of this unusual creature, so he (*send*) _____ his men ashore to ask the native inhabitants. When the natives (*ask*) _____ to name the animal, they said, "Kangaroo." The sailors, of course, believed "kangaroo" was the animal's name. Years later, the truth (*discover*) _____. "Kangaroo" means "I don't understand." But today the animal (*call, still*) _____ a kangaroo in English.

7. A person named Carl Gauss (*recognize*) _____ as a mathematical genius at the age of 10. One day a professor decided to pose an arithmetic problem to Carl. Carl (*ask*) _____ to add up all the numbers from 1 to 100 (1 + 2 + 3 + 4 + 5, etc.). It (*take*) _____ him eight seconds to solve the problem. How?*

8. The avalanche (*occur*) _____ around ten in the morning on October 7. Six skiers (*cross*) _____ a steep slope when suddenly they (*sweep*) _____ off their feet by cascading snow. Back at the ski resort, an avalanche alert was sounded, and a rescue party (*leave*) _____ immediately. After several hours, all six skiers (*find*) _____. Four of them (*injure, seriously*) _____, but they were all alive. The rescue party (*take*) _____ the injured skiers down the mountain as quickly as they could.

---

*He knew that each pair of numbers—1 plus 100, 2 plus 99, 3 plus 98, and so on to 50 plus 51—equaled 101. So he multiplied 50 times 101 and came up with the answer: 5,050.

Directions: Use the PAST PARTICIPLE or the PRESENT PARTICIPLE of the given verbs to complete the sentences. Use each verb only one time.

breed	*finance*	*scrub*	✔ *thread*
broadcast	*lean*	*shove*	*wind*
drag	*mine*	*smuggle*	
expose	✔ *redecorate*	*stretch*	

1. The Clarks' living room is being ___**redecorated**___ in blue and white. They want it to look nice for their daughter's wedding reception.

2. Jack pricked his finger while he was ___**threading**___ a needle.

3. The police talked to an informant. According to him, the illegal drugs had been _____ into the country in a private airplane.

4. The logging industry in that country still uses animal power. After the trees are cut down, the logs are _____ to the central camp by elephants.

5. On your trip to Tahiti, you will be _____ to many interesting customs, delicious food, and delightful people.

6. My hands and knees got sore while I was _____ the floor with soap and water.

7. The old clock wasn't ticking because it hadn't been _____. Someone forgot to do it.

8. The news of the victory was _____ throughout the country over the radio and television. Everyone heard about it almost as soon as it happened.

9. The bus was extremely crowded. I was _____ this way and that by the other passengers every time the bus turned a corner.

10. Oil exploration costs a lot of money. The explorations in the southern part of the country are being _____ by the government.

11. Frank was resting. He had been _____ back on his chair for several minutes with his eyes closed when he heard a knock on the door.

12. Gold is _____ in several countries. The nugget that Elena is wearing came from Brazil.

13. We couldn't enter the street. A rope had been _____ across the street.

14. Arabian horses are _____ at the Bar X ranch. They are quite expensive.

◇ **PRACTICE 13—GUIDED STUDY:** Present participle vs. past participle.
(Charts 1-2 and 3-1 → 3-3)

Directions: Use the PAST PARTICIPLE or the PRESENT PARTICIPLE of the given verbs to complete the sentences. Use each verb only one time.

bill	erase	✔ photograph	rub
destroy	✔ memorize	predict	vaccinate
equip	perform	rehearse	whisper

1. The vocabulary list had been ____*memorized*____ by all of the students, and each one scored over 90 percent on the exam.

2. Shhhh. Don't move. Don is ____*photographing*____ that deer, and we don't want to scare it off.

3. You'll want to buy this typewriter. It has been _____ with all of the latest accessories, including a 5,000-character storage memory.

4. The earthquake that struck the village was terrible. About 75 percent of the buildings were completely _____ within 2 minutes.

5. Little Jackie was _____ her eyes because she was sleepy.

6. Anna and Susie didn't hear what the teacher said because they were _____ to each other in the back of the classroom about the new boy in fifth grade.

7. Paul drew a funny picture of the teacher on the board, but it had been _____ before she entered the classroom.

8. The dance company is having a successful tour of the United States. Their dances will have been _____ over 500 times before they return to Senegal.

9. The National Weather Service is _____ another heat wave in the coming month. I hope they're wrong.

10. Robert and Julia had been _____ against cholera before they went abroad. They traveled without worrying about becoming infected.

11. When I went to the school auditorium, the children were _____ their musical play. The play is going to be presented this coming Friday at 7:00 P.M.

12. Carl spent two hours at the dentist's office today having some fillings put in. He will be _____ for the dental work at the end of the month.

◇ **PRACTICE 14—SELFSTUDY:** Passive modals. (Chart 3-4)

Directions: Change the following active sentences to the passive.

1. People should save pandas from extinction. → *Pandas should be saved from extinction.*

2. People must obey all traffic laws.

3. Someone ought to repair this broken window.

4. Someone should have supplied the hotel guests with clean towels.

5. Someone had better take this garbage to the dump soon.

6. People can pick tomatoes before they are completely ripe.

7. Someone is supposed to divide the profits among the shareholders.

8. Someone must have hurt Bob's feelings.

9. Someone has to finish this work today.

10. Someone ought to have reported the accident to the police.

11. You shouldn't put bananas in the freezer.

◇ **PRACTICE 15—SELFSTUDY: Passive modals. (Chart 3-4)**

Directions: Complete the sentences with the appropriate forms of the verbs in the list. Use each verb only one time. Some of the sentences are active and some are passive.

consider	*pollute*	*sew*	*whisper*
cost	*read*	*sign*	*wrap*
discover	✔ *repeat*	✔ *tell*	
forget	*replace*	*wear*	

1. Jack has a right to know. He ought to __*be told*__ the news immediately. If you don't do it, I will.

2. I have no patience with gossips. What I told Bill was a secret. He shouldn't have __*repeated*__ it to you.

3. Use this brown paper and tape. A package has to _____ carefully before it is mailed. Otherwise, the post office won't send it.

4. I don't know why Jessica wasn't at the meeting. She must have _____ about it. Next time there's a meeting, I'll be sure to remind her about it.

5. The ancient ruins may have _____ as early as 1792. The historical record is difficult to interpret.

6. You should _____ this button back on right away—before you lose it. Here's a needle and thread.

7. This burnt out light bulb should have _____ days ago. There are some new bulbs in the green cabinet. Could you get one for me?

8. Did you know that Sylvia bought a new sports car? I don't know how much she paid for it, and of course it's none of my business, but it must have _____ her a lot of money.

9. Shhhh. Let's not talk so loudly. We don't want to awaken the baby. We'd better _____.

10. You'd better not drink that river water. It could _____.

11. We have no choice in the matter. I know Tommy wants to spend the night outside in a tent with his friends, but he's sick. His well-being must _____ above all else. We have to tell him he can't do it.

12. While you are working here, you are never to greet the public in your everyday clothes. When you are on duty, your uniform must _____ at all times.

13. Your passport is supposed to _____. It is invalid without your signature.

14. I think everyone should _____ this paperback on the economic crisis. It has information that everyone should have.

◇ **PRACTICE 16—GUIDED STUDY: Passive modals. (Chart 3-4)**

Directions: Complete the sentences with the appropriate forms of the verbs in the list. Use each verb only one time. Some of the sentences are active and some are passive.

distinguish	✔ *obtain*	*scrub*	*vaccinate*
eat	*participate*	*stop*	*win*
establish	*reply*	*teach*	
kill	*revise*	*trade*	

1. A driver's license can ___**be obtained**___ from the Licensing Bureau at the corner of Pine Street and 5th Avenue.

2. Sam Smith was awarded the prize, but it should have _____ by Jennifer Watson. Her drawing was much better than his in my opinion.

3. Surgeons must _____ their hands thoroughly with disinfectant soap and hot water before they enter the operating room.

4. What are you talking about? You can't have _____ against the common cold. Small pox, maybe—but not the common cold.

5. A parrot can _____ to say words. I know a parrot that can say, "Me want food." Her grammar isn't very good, but she often manages to get something to eat.

HELLO, ME WANT FOOD.
HELLO, ME WANT FOOD.

6. When Mr. Brown said "How do you do?", you should have _____ by saying "How do you do?" I know that's not an answer to a question, but that's the way people talk when they greet each other.

7. I shouldn't have _____ by the police. I'm sure I wasn't speeding, but I got a ticket anyway.

8. Maria's composition was quite good, but it still had to _____. Her introduction didn't clearly state her thesis, and some of the ideas she presented weren't supported by specifics.

9. If you don't want to work tonight, you ought to _____ work shifts with Emily. She can work for you tonight, and you can work for her tomorrow night. The boss doesn't mind as long as someone is there to serve the food.

10. The games are open to anyone who wants to join in. Everyone can _____ in them. You don't have to sign up first. We welcome all players.

11. A university may _____ in outer space before long. Ideas for such a university are presently in the planning stage.

12. Your body needs lots of vitamins and minerals. You should _____ more salads and less junk food in the future.

13. A bald eagle can _____ from other large birds by its white head and white tail.

14. Some ranchers still believe that bald eagles must _____ to protect their livestock. Research has shown, however, that eagles do little if any damage to a rancher's stock. Today eagles are a protected species. The sight of a bald eagle soaring over water and trees fills one with awe and wonder at the beauty of nature.

Directions: Complete the sentences with the verbs in the list. Use the SIMPLE PRESENT. Use each verb only one time.

bury	cover	✔ excite	insure
close	crack	exhaust	pollute
confuse	dress	finish	stick

1. The children _____ **are excited** _____ about going to the circus. They're looking forward to seeing the elephants, the clowns, and the acrobats.

2. Three of the children have the measles. Their bodies _____ with red spots. They also have fevers.

3. A: What happened to this mirror? It _____.

   B: So it is. Someone must have dropped it.

4. The kids _____ from playing soccer all afternoon. They should rest for a while now.

5. _____ you _____ with that novel yet? I'd like to borrow it to read over the weekend.

6. A: I heard that a burglar broke into your house and stole all of your jewelry!

   B: Yes, and I feel terrible about it. Some of it was my grandmother's and can't be replaced. But at least all of it _____, and I'll be reimbursed for its value. It's still not the same as having the jewelry, though.

7. You shouldn't eat any of the fish from that river. The river _____ with chemical wastes from the factory upstream.

8. A: I'm going over to the theater to get tickets for the next concert.

   B: The ticket booth _____ until 6:00 P.M. You'll have to go there after six to get the tickets.

9. What's wrong with this drawer? I can't pull it open. It _____.

10. George _____ in his best suit today because he has an important interview this afternoon.

11. Douglas gave me one set of directions to their house, and Ann gave me a different set of directions. Needless to say, I _____ very _____. I hope we don't get lost on the way.

12. I know the scissors are somewhere on this desk. I think they _____ somewhere under these piles of papers.

◇ **PRACTICE 18—GUIDED STUDY: Stative passive. (Chart 3-5)**

Directions: Complete the sentences with the appropriate form of the verbs in the list. Use the SIMPLE PRESENT. Use each verb only one time.

acquaint	*equip*	*locate*	*schedule*
cancel	*forbid*	*make*	*summarize*
clog	*list*	*overdraw*	*wrinkle*

1. Maria's family lives in New York City, and her husband's family lives in Philadelphia. They would like to live in a city which _____ between the two so that they can visit their relatives frequently.

2. Robert wrote a very good, well-organized composition. The introduction tells the reader what the composition is about, and the last paragraph reviews all of his main points. His conclusions _____ in the last paragraph.

3. I don't know how, but I've lost my brother's new telephone number. Unfortunately, it _____ not _____, so I can't look it up in the directory. I'll have to call my mother and get it from her.

4. We can't climb over the fence to walk in that field. The sign says: "Trespassing _____ _____. Violators will be prosecuted."

5. I _____ not _____ with our new neighbors. They just moved in last week, and I haven't had the opportunity to introduce myself.

6. Your dental appointment _____ for 10:00 on Saturday. Please give us 24-hour notice if you need to cancel it.

7. I have to deposit some money in the bank immediately or I'm in big trouble. I've written too many checks and there's not enough money to cover them. My bank account _____ _____.

8. Good news! Our meeting _____. Now we can go to the beach after work instead of spending the evening at a meeting.

9. I can't wear this blouse because it _____. I'd have to iron it, and I don't have time.

10. Some new automobiles _____ with air bags as well as seat belts. The air bags provide additional protection in case of an accident.

11. That table _____ of plastic, not wood. The manufacturer certainly did a good job of imitating the look of wood.

12. It takes a long time for the water to go down the drain in my kitchen sink. I think the drain _____ with grease and food particles. I'd better call the plumber tomorrow.

◇ PRACTICE 19—SELFSTUDY: Stative passive + prepositions. (Chart 3-5 and Appendix 2)

Directions: Complete the sentences with appropriate PREPOSITIONS.

1. Our high-school soccer team was very excited ___*about*___ going to the national finals.

2. I'm not acquainted _____ that man. Do you know him?

3. Mark Twain is known _____ his stories about life on the Mississippi.

4. A person who is addicted _____ drugs needs professional medical help.

5. This apartment comes furnished _____ only a stove and refrigerator.

6. Mr. Bellamy is discriminated _____ because of his age. When he applies for a job, he gets turned down as soon as they learn he is 61 years old.

7. Jack is married _____ Joan.

8. Could I please have the dictionary when you are finished _____ it?

9. A: Aren't you ready yet? We have to be at the ferry dock at 7:45.

   B: We'll never make it. I'm still dressed _____ my pajamas.

10. My car is equipped _____ air conditioning and a sun roof.

11. The schoolchildren were exposed _____ measles by a student who had them.

12. Gandhi was committed _____ nonviolence. He believed in it all of his life.

13. The boss is so convinced _____ Jean's ability that he's paying her more money than he paid the previous employee.

14. The large table was covered _____ every kind of food you could imagine.

15. Barbara turned off the TV because she was tired _____ listening to the news.

16. Victor is blessed _____ a good sense of humor, which has helped him get out of some very difficult situations.

17. A: Are the choices in this restaurant limited _____ pizza and sandwiches?

    B: No. If you're interested _____ other dishes, take a look at the back page of the menu.

18. A: Are you disappointed _____ the color of this room? We could repaint it.

    B: I think I'm satisfied _____ it the way it is. What do you think?

19. A: Are you in favor of nuclear disarmament, or are you opposed _____ it?

    B: I'm in favor of it. I'm terrified _____ the possibility of an accidental nuclear war. My wife, however, is against disarmament.

◇ PRACTICE 20—SELFSTUDY: Stative passive + prepositions. (Chart 3-5 and Appendix 2)

Directions: Complete the sentences with appropriate PREPOSITIONS.

1. The department store was filled _____ toys for the holiday sale.

2. George Washington, the first president of the United States, is remembered _____ his strong leadership during the Revolutionary War.

3. John's bald head is protected _____ the hot sun. He's wearing a straw hat.

4. The store was crowded _____ last-minute shoppers on the eve of the holiday.

5. I think you're involved _____ too many activities. You don't have enough time to spend with your family.

6. Your leg bone is connected _____ your hip bone.

7. Zoology is more closely related _____ biology than it is to botany.

8. Their apartment is always messy. It's cluttered _____ newspapers, books, clothes, and dirty dishes.

9. I'm annoyed _____ my boss. He scheduled a meeting for an hour beginning at ten o'clock, the same time I was planning to see a client.

10. As soon as you are done _____ the dictionary, I'd like to use it.

11. Last month, little Billy was bitten by a dog. Now he's scared _____ every dog he sees.

12. Don't leave those seedlings outside tonight. If they're exposed _____ temperatures below freezing, they'll die.

13. An interior decorator makes certain that the color of the walls is coordinated _____ the color of the carpets and window coverings.

14. Carol is engaged _____ Larry. Their marriage is planned for May 3.

15. We finished packing our sleeping bags, tent, first-aid kit, food, and warm clothes. We're finally prepared _____ our camping trip.

16. A: Why are you so upset _____ the children?

    B: They didn't call me when they missed their school bus, and I got very worried.

17. I was very disappointed _____ that movie. The whole first hour was devoted _____ historical background with a cast of thousands fighting endless battles. I was bored _____ it before the plot took shape.

18. A: Are you still associated _____ the International Red Cross?

    B: I was, until this year. Are you interested _____ working with them?

    A: I think I'd like to. They're dedicated _____ helping people in time of crisis, and I admire the work they've done. Can you get me some information?

◇ PRACTICE 21—GUIDED STUDY: Present vs. past participles. (Charts 1-2, 3-5, and Appendix 2)

Directions: Complete the sentences with the verbs in the list. Use the PRESENT PARTICIPLE or the PAST PARTICIPLE. Include a PREPOSITION if necessary. Use each verb only one time.

accompany	compose	✔ explain	limit
annoy	✔ concern	involve	provide
bless	connect	know	satisfy
blow	cross	laugh	

1. I am _____*concerned about*_____ your health. You're not taking good care of yourself.

2. Shhh! The teacher is _____*explaining*_____ the assignment, and I want to hear what he's saying.

3. Paris is famous for the Eiffel Tower. Bangkok is _____ its floating market, which is a favorite tourist attraction.

4. In elementary school, all of the children are _____ textbooks. They don't have to buy their own.

5. Everyone is _____ hard because Don is telling a very funny story.

6. Diane is a perfectionist when it comes to developing her photographs. She's been in the darkroom for hours and won't come out until she is completely _____ _____ the prints.

7. The Atlantic Ocean is _____ the Pacific Ocean by the Panama Canal. Ships can go from one ocean to the other without having to sail around the southern tip of South America.

8. While I was _____ the street, a car came out of nowhere and almost hit me.

9. Most teenagers are very busy after school. They are _____ many extracurricular activities, such as sports and special interest clubs.

10. An alloy is a metal compound that is _____ two or more metals.

11. Mrs. Hill doesn't have to travel alone. Her daughter is _____ her to Rome.

12. We are fortunate people. We are _____ a happy home and good health. We have many things to be thankful for.

13. The enrollment in that class is _____ 25 students. You'd better sign up for it early. Otherwise, you won't be able to get in.

14. My neighbors are quite inconsiderate. They make so much noise that I can't get to sleep at night. I am very _____ them.

15. The weather was awful. It was raining so hard it was impossible to see across the valley, and the wind was _____ so hard that it was difficult to walk.

◇ PRACTICE 22—SELFSTUDY: The passive with *get*. (Chart 3-6)

Directions: Complete the sentences by using an appropriate form of *get* and the PAST PARTICIPLE of the verbs in the list.

break	hurt	start	✔ tear
bury	lose	stick	worry
hire	soak		

1. I had a terrible day. First the heel of my shoe broke off, then my dress __*got torn*__ in the elevator door. I'm glad the day is over!

2. Oh! Look at that beautiful vase on the floor. How did it _____?

3. A: You're late. What happened?

   B: We _____. We took the wrong exit from the highway, and it took a long time to figure out where we were.

4. A: I really need a job.

   B: Why don't you apply for a job at the fast-food restaurant? They're looking for help. I'm sure you'll _____.

5. A: Did Susan _____ when she fell down the stairs?

   B: Not badly. Just a few bumps and bruises. She'll be fine.

6. A: You're here! I _____ about you. What happened that made you so late?

   B: I couldn't start my car. The battery was dead.

7. Maureen _____ thoroughly _____ when her canoe tipped over and she fell into the river. She looked like a drowned rat.

8. In two weeks the school term will be finished. I'd better _____ on my term paper before it's too late. I've been procrastinating too long.

9. It was a real tragedy. The rains were torrential, and the mudslide completely covered everything. Three houses _____ in the mud when it rolled down the hillside. We could barely see the rooftops.

10. A: I heard about your embarrassing situation last night.

    B: It was awful! I put my big toe in the faucet while I was taking a bath, and it _____! I couldn't pull it out no matter how hard I tried.

◇ PRACTICE 23—GUIDED STUDY: The passive with *get*. (Chart 3-6)

Directions: Complete the sentences by using an appropriate form of ***get*** and the PAST PARTICIPLE of the verbs in the list.

accept	*dress*	*embarrass*	*invite*
catch	*elect*	*fire*	*mug*
cheat	*electrocute*	✔ *hit*	*ruin*

1. I shouldn't have parked my car near the construction site. It _____ ***got hit*** _____ by falling rocks. Now it's full of dents and scratches.

2. Tom has applied to three top universities. Since he's an excellent student, I'm sure he'll

_____ by at least one of them. If he doesn't, there are other good

schools he can attend.

3. Alex thought he had gotten a good deal when he bought a diamond ring from some guy on the

street, but the "stone" turned out to be glass and was practically worthless. Alex

_____ .

4. A: I can't believe Paul _____ from his job. I thought he was doing well.

B: He was, but then he had a major disagreement with his boss, and tempers were flying. I

hope he gets his job back.

5. A: Let's take the subway.

B: Not me. The last time I was on the subway, I _____ . A man

knocked me down and stole my wallet.

6. A: Did you _____ to the Saunder's dinner party tonight?

B: Yes, but I can't go.

7. A: You're all out of breath!

B: I was late getting home and had to _____ quickly. Then I ran all the

way over here.

A: Well, that explains why your collar is up and your tie is crooked.

8. The animal was running through the woods when it suddenly _____ in

the hunter's trap.

9. It was a close election. The new president _____ by a very small

margin.

10. What are you doing?!! Don't let the cord to your electric hair dryer fall into the sink. You'll

_____ !

11. We managed to save some of the furniture, but many of our things _____

when the floodwaters poured into our house.

12. During the school play, little Annie _____ when she couldn't

remember the lines she was supposed to say.

◇ PRACTICE 24—SELFSTUDY: Participial adjectives. (Chart 3-7)

Directions: Complete the sentences with the correct form (PRESENT or PAST PARTICIPLE) of
the italicized word.

1. The book *interests* me. (a) It is an ___*interesting*___ book. (b) I am ___*interested*___ in it.

2. That chemical *irritates* your skin. (a) The chemical is _____ . (b) Your

skin is _____ .

3. The trip *tired* everybody. (a) Everyone was _____ . (b) The trip was _____ .

4. Ann *boiled* an egg. (a) She took the egg out of the _____ water. (b) She had a

_____ egg for breakfast.

5. The news *upset* us.   (a) We were _____.   (b) The news was _____.

6. The instructions on the box for assembling the tool *confuse* me.   (a) They are

_____.   (b) I am thoroughly _____.

7. Bob's grades *disappointed* his parents.   (a) His grades were _____.

(b) His parents were _____.

8. My father often *reassured* me.   (a) He was a very _____ person.   (b) I

always felt _____ when I was around him.

9. I waited for two hours to see the doctor, and it really *frustrated* me!   (a) Long waits such as

that can be very _____.   (b) I was _____.

10. Anna has a noise in her car that *disturbs* her.   (a) It is a _____ noise.

(b) She is _____ when she hears it.

11. Jessica's arguments *convinced* us.   (a) She presented _____ arguments.

(b) We were _____.

12. The tender love story *moved* the audience.   (a) It was a _____ story.   (b) The

audience felt _____.

13. Their behavior *shocked* us.   (a) It was _____ behavior.   (b) We were

_____.

14. The sad movie *depressed* me.   (a) I was _____.   (b) It was a

_____ movie.

15. The unkind teacher's harsh words *humiliated* the student.   (a) The _____

student hung his head in shame.   (b) The student never forgot that _____

experience.

16. The newspaper account of the new medical discovery *intrigued* me.   (a) It was an

_____ account.   (b) Other _____ people wrote the

newspaper to get more information.

◇ **PRACTICE 25—SELFSTUDY: Participial adjectives. (Chart 3-7)**

Directions: Complete the sentences with the correct form of the word in parentheses.

1. (*Pollute*) **Polluted** water is not safe for drinking.

2. I don't have any furniture of my own. Do you know where I can rent a (*furnish*)

_____ apartment?

3. The equator is the (*divide*) _____ line between the Northern and Southern

Hemispheres.

4. The poor people who live in shacks south of the city don't have (*run*) _____

water.

5. No one may attend the lecture except (*invite*) _____ guests.

6. We all expect our (*elect*) _____ officials to be honest.

7. The (*suggest*) _____ remedy for the common cold is to rest and to drink plenty of fluids.

8. Because we have a (*write*) _____ agreement, our landlord won't be able to raise our rent for two years.

9. After an (*exhaust*) _____ trip of twelve hours, Jason fell asleep at the dinner table.

10. There are many (*stimulate*) _____ activities in a large city.

11. The anthropologist recorded the tribe's (*speak*) _____ language with a small tape recorder.

12. I like to hear the sound of gently (*fall*) _____ rain.

13. (*Freeze*) _____ fish is as nutritious as fresh fish, but it doesn't taste quite as good.

14. The (*invade*) _____ army plundered the villages of food and valuables.

15. Skydiving is a (*thrill*) _____ experience.

◇ **PRACTICE 26—GUIDED STUDY: Participial adjectives. (Chart 3-7)**

Directions: Complete the sentences with the correct form of the word in parentheses.

1. The invention of the (*print*) _____ press was one of the most important events in the history of the world.

2. (*Experience*) _____ travelers pack lightly. They carry little more than necessities.

3. Ben's tasteless jokes didn't produce the (*intend*) _____ effect. Instead, his guests were offended.

4. The professor dispelled the tense atmosphere in the classroom by beginning her lecture with some (*amuse*) _____ anecdotes.

5. That country is highly industrialized but has very little arable land. Its economy depends upon the export of various (*manufacture*) _____ goods in exchange for imported agricultural products.

6. When I get home from work, I'm going to take a long, (*relax*) _____ bath.

7. The psychologist spoke to us about some of the (*amaze*) _____ coincidences in the lives of twins living apart from each other from birth.

8. The scientist reviewed all of his procedures for the experiment after the (*expect*) _____ results did not occur.

9. When Brenda heard the news of the (*approach*) _____ hurricane, she bought flashlight batteries, candles, and canned food to prepare for it.

10. Bright children have (*inquire*) _____ minds.

11. The game was played in our stadium. The (*visit*) _____ team scored the (*win*) _____ goal in the last seconds of the soccer game. Nevertheless, the (*disappoint*) _____ fans continued to cheer our team.

12. I heard some (*encourage*) _____ news.

13. Sally spends her vacations in the mountains. The fresh air invigorates her. She likes the cool, (*invigorate*) _____ air.

14. Waste from the factory poured into the river and contaminated it. Some of the villagers got sick from eating (*contaminate*) _____ fish.

◇ **PRACTICE 27—GUIDED STUDY:** Verb form review, active and passive. (Chapters 1 and 3)

Directions: Complete the sentences with the words in parentheses.

1. Only coffee and dessert (*serve*) __**were served**__ at the reception yesterday.

2. Kim wants very badly to make the Olympic team next year. She (*train*) __**has been training**__ hard for the last two years.

3. I've looked in my purse, on the dresser, in my coat pocket, and on all of the tables in the house, but I can't find my keys anywhere. They (*lose*) _____.

4. Some people in my country don't take politics seriously. In a recent parliamentary election, a cartoon character named Donald Duck (*receive*) _____ 291 votes.

5. According to present company policy, bonuses for the most sales (*give*) _____ to the sales staff at the end of July every year.

6. According to our Constitution, everyone is equal. But in truth, some minorities (*discriminate*) _____ against in our country. In the last 20 years, new laws (*enact*) _____ to help ensure equality in housing and job opportunities.

7. Mark is a genius. By the time he graduated, he (*offer*) _____ jobs by a dozen computer companies.

8. When I (*finish*) _____ my work, I'm going to take a walk.

9. After the test papers (*return*) _____ to the students in class tomorrow, the students (*give*) _____ their next assignment.

10. Since the beginning of the modern industrial age, many of the natural habitats of plants and animals (*destroy*) _____ by industrial development and pollution.

11. The Olympic Games began in 776 B.C. in Olympia, a small town in Greece. At that time, only Greeks (*allow*) _____ to compete in them.

12. I (*fool, not*) _____ when Linda told us she'd won a million dollars at the racetrack. I knew she was only kidding.

13. There are certain (*establish*) _____ procedures that must (*follow*) _____ in conducting a scientific experiment.

14. Due to his abrasive, (*irritate*) _____ manner, Mr. Morrow has difficulty getting along with his co-workers. He (*replace*) _____ by Mr. Han next month as the co-ordinator of the production plans.

15. Ever since it (*build*) _____ three centuries ago, the Taj Mahal in Agra (*describe, often*) _____ as the most beautiful building in the world. It (*design*) _____ by a Turkish architect, and it (*take*) _____ 20,000 workers 20 years to complete it.

16. The photography competition that is taking place at the art museum today (*judge*) _____ by three well-known photographers. I've entered three of my pictures and have my fingers crossed. The results (*announce*) _____ later this afternoon.

17. When Jake put a coin in the (*vend*) _____ machine for a can of soda pop, nothing came out. So in a fit of temper, he (*kick*) _____ it hard. Suddenly, it (*fall*) _____ over, right on top of Jake, who (*injure, seriously*) _____. Jake (*end*) _____ up in the hospital for three weeks, and today he (*wear, still*) _____ a cast on his arm. I bet that's the last time he ever kicks a (*vend*) _____ machine.

18. I have a serious problem with my (*propose*) _____ class schedule this semester. The chemistry class that I need for my science requirement (*offer, not*) _____ _____ this semester. I don't know what to do. I need that class in order to graduate in June.

19. A: Arthur (*jog*) _____ for a full hour. He must be tired.

    B: Why is he jogging so much these days?

    A: He (*plan*) _____ to run in the 10k race in Chicago next month, and he wants to be ready for it.

20. A census is a survey of the population of a country. In the United States, a population census (*conduct*) _____ by the government every ten years. Questionnaires (*send*) _____ to every household in the country. People (*ask*) _____ about such things as their employment, education, housing, and family size. After the information (*collect*) _____, it (*publish*) _____ by the Census Bureau. Many government agencies (*use*) _____ this information to make plans for the future about housing, agriculture, urban development, public transportation, and schools.

◇ PRACTICE 28—SELFSTUDY: Error analysis. (Chapter 3)

Directions: Find and correct the errors in the following sentences.

1. The children were frightening by the thunder and lightning.
2. Two people got hurted in the accident and were took to the hospital by an ambulance.
3. The movie was so bored that we fell asleep after an hour.
4. The students helped by the clear explanation that the teacher gave.
5. That alloy is composing by iron and tin.
6. The winner of the race hasn't been announcing yet.
7. If you are interesting in modern art, you should see the new exhibit at the museum. It is fascinated.
8. Progress is been made every day.
9. When, where, and by whom has the automobile invented?
10. My brother and I have always been interesting in learning more about our family history.
11. I am not agree with you, and I don't think you'll ever be convince me.
12. Each assembly kit is accompany by detailed instructions.
13. Arthur was giving an award by the city for all of his efforts in crime prevention.
14. It was late, and I was getting very worry about my son.
15. The problem was very puzzled. I couldn't figure it out.
16. Many strange things were happened last night.

◇ PRACTICE 29—GUIDED STUDY: Writing.

Directions: In writing, describe how something is made. Choose one of the following:

1. Use a reference book such as an encyclopedia to find out how something is made, and then summarize this information. It's not necessary to get into technical details. Read about the process and then describe it in your own words. *Possible subjects:* paper, a candle, a pencil, glass, steel, silk thread, bronze, leather, etc.
2. Write about something you know how to make. *Possible subjects:* a kite, a ceramic pot, a bookcase, a sweater, a bead necklace, a special decoration, a special kind of food, etc.

Notice the use of the passive in the following example.

Paper is a common material that **is used** throughout the world. It **has been made** from various plants, such as rice and papyrus, and used **to be made** by hand. Today wood is the chief source of paper, and most of the work **is done** by machines. Paper **can be made** from wood pulp by either a mechanical or a chemical process.

In the mechanical process, the wood **is ground** into small chips. During the grinding, it **is sprayed** with water to keep it from burning from the friction of the grinder. Then the chips **are soaked** in water.

In the chemical process, first the wood **is washed**, and then it **is cut** into small pieces by a chipping machine. The wood **is** then **cooked** in certain chemicals. After cooking, the wood **is washed** to get rid of the chemicals.

The pulp that results from either the mechanical or chemical process **is** then **drained** to form a thick mass. Next it **is bleached** in chlorine and then thoroughly **washed** again. Then the pulp **is put** through a machine that squeezes the water out and forms the pulp into long sheets. Next the pulp sheets pass through a drier and a press. Then they **are wound** into rolls.

Remember: You are writing a general description of how something is made. You are not giving your reader instructions to follow. Do not write in the second person (*e.g., If you want to make paper, first you grind the wood into small chips. Be sure to spray the chips during the grinding so they don't burn. Then you soak the chips in water.*). Write a description, not instructions.

◇ PRACTICE TEST A—SELFSTUDY: The passive. (Chapter 3)

Directions: Choose the correct answer.
Example:

___**D**___ *Ms. Haugen _____ at the Ajax Company.*
          A. is employing   *B. employed*   *C. employing*   *D. is employed*

_____ 1. I still can't believe it! My bicycle _____ last night.
          A. was stolen   B. was stealing   C. stolen   D. stole

_____ 2. The current constitutional problem is _____ by the top legal minds in the country.
          A. studying   B. being studying   C. being studied   D. been studied

_____ 3. Something funny _____ in class yesterday.
          A. happened   B. was happened   C. happens   D. is happened

_____ 4. The child's arm was swollen because he _____ by a bee.
   A. stung   B. had stung
   C. had been stung   D. had being stung

_____ 5. Today, many serious childhood diseases _____ by early immunization.
   A. are preventing   B. can prevent
   C. prevent   D. can be prevented

_____ 6. I _____ with you on that subject.
   A. am agree   B. am agreed   C. agreeing   D. agree

_____ 7. Many U.S. automobiles _____ in Detroit, Michigan.
   A. manufacture   B. have manufactured
   C. are manufactured   D. are manufacturing

_____ 8. Let's go ahead and do it now. Nothing _____ by waiting.
   A. accomplishes   B. accomplished
   C. has accomplished   D. will be accomplished

_____ 9. "When _____?"
   "In 1928."
   A. penicillin was discovered   B. did penicillin discovered
   C. was penicillin discovered   D. did penicillin discover

_____ 10. In recent years, the government has imposed pollution controls on automobile
   manufacturers. Both domestic and imported automobiles must _____ anti-pollution
   devices.
   A. equip with   B. be equipped with
   C. equip by   D. be equipped by

_____ 11. A shortage of water is a problem in many parts of the world. In some areas, water _____
   from the ground faster than nature can replenish the supply.
   A. is being taken   B. has been taking
   C. is taking   D. has taken

_____ 12. Vitamin C _____ by the human body. It gets into the blood stream quickly.
   A. absorbs easily   B. is easily absorbing
   C. is easily absorbed   D. absorbed easily

_____ 13. "When can I have my car back?"
   "I think it'll _____ late this afternoon."
   A. finish   B. be finished   C. have finished   D. be finish

_____ 14. I didn't think my interview went very well, but I guess it must have. Despite all my
   anxiety, I _____ for the job I wanted. I'm really going to work hard to justify their
   confidence.
   A. was hiring   B. hired   C. got hiring   D. got hired

_____ 15. My country _____ the pursuit of world peace.
   A. is dedicating to   B. is dedicated to
   C. is dedicating by   D. is dedicated by

_____ 16. About 15,000 years ago, northern Wisconsin _____ under ice a mile deep.
   A. buried   B. was burying   C. was buried   D. had buried

_____ 17. Ed was new on the job, but he quickly fit himself into the _____ routine of the office.
   A. established   B. establishing   C. establishes   D. establish

_____ 18. The Mayan Indians _____ an accurate and sophisticated calendar more than seven
   centuries ago.
   A. were developed   B. developed
   C. are developed   D. have been developed

_____ 19. George is _____ Lisa.
        A. marry with   B. marry to   C. married with   D. married to

_____ 20. The rescuers _____ for their bravery and fortitude in locating the lost mountain climbers.
        A. were praised   B. praised   C. were praising   D. praising

◇ PRACTICE TEST B—GUIDED STUDY: The passive. (Chapter 3)

Directions: Choose the correct answer.

Example:

__D__ _Ms. Haugen _____ at the Ajax Company._
        A. is employing   _B. employed_   _C. employing_   _D. is employed_

_____ 1. "Can't we do something about the situation?"
     "Something _____ right now."
        A. is doing   B. is done
        C. is being done   D. has been doing

_____ 2. "Are you interested in scuba diving?"
     "Very. Undersea life is _____."
        A. fascinated   B. fascinating
        C. being fascinating   D. being fascinated

_____ 3. The university _____ by private funds as well as by tuition income and grants.
        A. is supported   B. supports   C. is supporting   D. has supported

_____ 4. My car made strange noises, sputtered to a stop, and then wouldn't start again. Fortunately, the mechanic at my garage _____ the source of the problem.
        A. was discover   B. discovered
        C. was discovered   D. has been discovered

_____ 5. "Ms. Jones, please type those letters before noon."
     "They've already _____, sir. They're on your desk."
        A. typed   B. been typed
        C. being typed   D. been being typed

_____ 6. "Has the committee made its decision yet?"
     "Not yet. They are still _____ the proposal."
        A. considering   B. been considered
        C. being considered   D. considered

_____ 7. In some rural areas of the United States, health care _____ by only a small number of doctors, nurses, and other health professionals. It's often more than they can handle.
        A. is providing   B. is being provided
        C. provides   D. provided

_____ 8. "How did that window _____?"
     "I don't know."
        A. get broken   B. broke   C. got broken   D. broken

_____ 9. Renoir is one of the most popular French impressionist painters. His paintings _____ masterpieces all over the world.
        A. had considered   B. are considering
        C. are considered   D. consider

_____ 10. As the fairy tale goes, the prince _____ into a frog by an evil magician, and only a kiss from a beautiful princess could restore him to his original state.
    A. turned   B. was turning
    C. was turned   D. had been turning

_____ 11. When I woke up and looked outside, the landscape had changed. The ground had been lightly _____ with a dusting of snow during the night.
    A. covering   B. cover   C. covers   D. covered

_____ 12. We can't even walk in this storm. Let's wait in the hallway where we'll be _____ the strong winds until things quiet down.
    A. protected from   B. protected by
    C. protecting from   D. protecting by

_____ 13. "_____ about the eight o'clock flight to Chicago?"
"Not yet."
    A. Has been an announcement made   B. Has an announcement made
    C. Has an announcement been made   D. Has been made an announcement

_____ 14. Last night a tornado swept through Rockville. It _____ everything in its path.
    A. destroyed   B. was destroyed
    C. was being destroyed   D. had been destroyed

_____ 15. Be sure to wash these vegetables thoroughly. A lot of pesticide residue _____ on unwashed produce.
    A. can find   B. can found   C. can be found   D. can be finding

_____ 16. The building of the bridge had been delayed for three years because of political problems on both sides of the river. Finally, it _____ because the public demanded action, and now many hours of driving have been saved for daily commuters.
    A. was constructed   B. gets constructed
    C. constructed   D. has constructed

_____ 17. On Friday afternoon before a three-day holiday weekend, the highways _____ people on their way out of the city.
    A. are crowding by   B. are being crowd with
    C. are crowded with   D. crowd by

_____ 18. Fortunately, the hospital's new air-conditioning system _____ when the first heat wave of the summer arrived.
    A. had installed   B. installed
    C. had been installed   D. had been installing

_____ 19. It's hard to believe that my application for a scholarship _____. I was sure I'd get it. I don't know now if I'll go to school next year.
    A. was denied   B. denied   C. was denying   D. has denied

_____ 20. The man died because medical help was not summoned. A doctor should _____ immediately.
    A. have called   B. been called
    C. called   D. have been called

CHAPTER 4
Gerunds and Infinitives

◇ **PRACTICE 1—SELFSTUDY:**   Gerunds as objects of prepositions. (Chart 4-2)

Directions: Complete the sentences with PREPOSITIONS followed by GERUNDS. Use the verbs in the given list. Use each verb only once.

✔ ask	*have*	*make*	*see*
break	*kill*	*open*	*talk*
finish	*lock*	*practice*	*wash*

1. Instead _____*of asking*_____ for help on each arithmetic problem, you should use your book and try to figure out the answers yourself.

2. I look forward _____ you the next time I'm in town. I'll be sure to let you know ahead of time so that we can plan to get together.

3. Alice told us that she was tired _____ the dishes every night.

4. The four-year-old was blamed _____ the glass candy dish.

5. Because of the bomb scare, no one was allowed in the building. People were prevented _____ the front door by a guard who was stationed there.

6. You should listen to other people instead _____ about yourself all the time.

7. What do you feel _____ for dinner? Does chicken and rice sound good?

8. Frank is an environmental conservationist who believes animals should be protected from hunters. He objects _____ wild animals for sport.

9. Please don't argue _____ your homework. Just do it.

10. Marie is responsible _____ all the doors and windows and _____ sure all the lights are turned off before she leaves work in the evening.

11. Mario spent all month preparing for the tennis match, but in spite _____ for many hours each day, he lost the match to Ivan.

◇ **PRACTICE 2—GUIDED STUDY: Gerunds as objects of prepositions. (Chart 4-2)**

Directions: Using the verbs in parentheses, complete the sentences with your own words.

1. (*help*)   I thanked my friend . . . *for helping me with my homework.*
2. (*collect*)   The treasurer is responsible . . . .
3. (*work*)   The employees objected . . . .
4. (*be*)   I apologized . . . .
5. (*win*)   Mark is capable . . . .
6. (*get*)   I'm not used . . . .
7. (*go to*)   The rainy weather prevented us . . . .
8. (*clean up*)   All of the children participated . . . .
9. (*enter*)   Unauthorized persons are prohibited . . . .
10. (*attend*)   She was excited . . . .
11. (*bring*)   I thanked the flight attendant . . . .
12. (*hire*)   Mr. Smith is opposed . . . .
13. (*have to do*) The students complained . . . .

◇ **PRACTICE 3—GUIDED STUDY: Verbs followed by gerunds. (Charts 4-3 and 4-4)**

Directions: Make sentences using the given verbs.
Examples:
    enjoy + watch → *Do you enjoy watching old movies on television?*
    mind + have to be → *I don't mind having to be in class at 8:00 A.M.*
    put off + pack → *Dan usually puts off packing his suitcase until the very last minute.*

1. talk about + take
2. avoid + eat
3. go + jog
4. finish + do
5. mind + have to stay
6. consider + go + swim
7. stop + cry

8. discuss + go + shop
9. mention + have to go
10. delay + put
11. suggest + change
12. keep + ask
13. quit + worry about
14. postpone + take

◇ **PRACTICE 4—SELFSTUDY: Gerund vs. infinitive. (Charts 4-1 → 4-5)**

Directions: Select the correct answer for each sentence.

__*B*__ 1. Whenever we met, Jack avoided _____ at me.
             A. to look   B. looking

_____ 2. Most people enjoy _____ to different parts of the world.
             A. to travel   B. traveling

_____ 3. Marjorie needs _____ another job. Her present company is going out of business.
             A. to find   B. finding

_____ 4. May I change the TV channel, or do you want _____ more of this program?
             A. to watch   B. watching

_____ 5. Joan is considering _____ her major from pre-med studies to psychology.
             A. to change   B. changing

_____ 6. Although Joe slammed on his brakes, he couldn't avoid _____ the small dog that suddenly darted out in front of his car.
    A. to hit   B. hitting

_____ 7. I hope _____ my autobiography before I die. Do you think anyone would read it?
    A. to write   B. writing

_____ 8. Joyce thanked us for _____ them to dinner and said that they wanted to have us over for dinner next week.
    A. to invite   B. inviting

_____ 9. If you delay _____ your bills, you will only incur more and more interest charges.
    A. to pay   B. paying

_____ 10. My lawyer advised me not _____ anything further about the accident.
    A. to say   B. saying

_____ 11. A procrastinator is one who habitually postpones _____ things—especially tasks that are unpleasant.
    A. to do   B. doing

_____ 12. You should plan _____ at the stadium early or you won't be able to get good seats.
    A. to arrive   B. arriving

_____ 13. My mom asked me _____ up some eggs at the supermarket on my way home from work.
    A. to pick   B. picking

_____ 14. Nobody has offered _____ the house next door, so I think they're going to lower the price.
    A. to buy   B. buying

_____ 15. The highway patrol advises _____ the old route through the city because the interstate highway is under major repairs.
    A. to take   B. taking

_____ 16. Would you mind _____ that apple for me? My arthritis is acting up in my right hand.
    A. to peel   B. peeling

_____ 17. Stop _____ me! I'll get everything finished before I go to bed.
    A. to nag   B. nagging

_____ 18. When the university suggested _____ the tuition again, the student senate protested vigorously.
    A. to raise   B. raising

_____ 19. Are we permitted _____ guests to the ceremony? I'd like to invite my friend to join us.
    A. to bring   B. bringing

_____ 20. The city council agreed _____ the architect's proposed design for a new parking garage.
    A. to accept   B. accepting

◇ PRACTICE 5—SELFSTUDY: Verbs followed by infinitives. (Chart 4-5)

Directions: Restate the given sentences. Choose the most appropriate reporting verb in parentheses. Make it active or passive as appropriate. Include an INFINITIVE in the completion and any other necessary words.

1. The teacher said to Jim, "Would you give your book to Mary, please?
   (ask, tell, order)
   → The teacher _____ _ask Jim to give_ _____ his book to Mary.

2. The sign said, "No parking in this area. Violators will be towed away."
   (*invite, warn, force*)
   → Drivers _____*were warned not to park*_____ in the area.

3. Before Bobby went to bed, his father said, "Don't forget to brush your teeth."
   (*invite, allow, remind*)
   → Before Bobby went to bed, his father _____
   his teeth.

4. Under the law, drivers and all passengers must wear seat belts while in a moving vehicle.
   (*encourage, require, permit*)
   → Drivers and passengers _____ seat belts while in
   a moving vehicle.

5. When I asked the nurse about my skin rash, she said, "You should consult a dermatologist."
   (*ask, permit, advise*)
   → The nurse _____ a dermatologist.

6. The fire chief said, "Everyone must leave the building immediately."
   (*order, remind, allow*)
   → Everyone _____ the building immediately.

7. The instructor said to the students, "You will have exactly one hour to complete the exam."
   (*order, expect, warn*)
   → The students _____ the exam in one
   hour.

8. Because he forgot last year, I told my husband several times that he should buy some flowers
   for his mother on Mother's Day.
   (*remind, require, allow*)
   → I _____ some flowers for his
   mother on Mother's Day.

9. My garage mechanic said, "You should get a tune-up every 5,000 miles."
   (*ask, order, advise*)
   → My garage mechanic _____ a tune-up every 5,000
   miles.

10. The factory manager said to the employees, "Do not come late. If you do, you will lose your
    jobs."
    (*ask, warn, encourage*)
    → The employees _____ late.

11. The sign on the side door says, "Do not enter," so we have to use a different door.
    (*ask, permit, force*)
    → Nobody _____ the side door.

12. The little girl said to her father, "Daddy, I really like this tricycle. Can we buy it?"
    (*require, ask, advise*)
    → The little girl _____ a tricycle for her.

13. We often told our grandfather, "Your experiences as a sailor in the navy were fascinating. You
    should write a book about them."
    (*remind, encourage, require*)
    → We _____ a book about his
    experiences in the navy.

14. The judge said to the defendant, "You must not shout in the courtroom again."
    (*ask, order, encourage*)
    → The defendant _____ in the courtroom again.

Directions: Report what the speakers say by using a verb from the following list and an INFINITIVE phrase. Use each verb in the list one time only. Make your sentence passive if the speaker is not specifically identified.

advise	✔ ask	invite	remind
allow	encourage	order	warn

1. During the water shortage, someone in authority said to the public, "Curtail your use of water as much as possible."
   → *During the water shortage, the public was asked to curtail its use of water as much as possible.*
2. Laura said to her roommate, "Don't forget to set your alarm clock for 6:00 A.M."
3. Mrs. Jones said to the children, "Each of you may have one piece of candy."
4. The doctor said to my father, "It would be best if you limited your sugar consumption."
5. My parents often said to me, "Good for you! It's good to be independent!"
6. Someone said to the children, "Don't swim in the lake without an adult present."
7. The police officer shouted to the reckless driver, "Pull over!"
8. Rose said to Gerald, "I'd like you to come to my house Sunday night to meet my parents."

◇ PRACTICE 7—SELFSTUDY: Gerund vs. infinitive. (Chart 4-6)

Directions: Choose the best answer or answers. In some cases, BOTH answers are correct.

__B__ 1. John was trying _____ the door with the wrong key.
    A. unlocking   B. to unlock

__A, B__ 2. The audience began _____ before the curtains closed.
    A. clapping   B. to clap

_____ 3. The soccer teams continued _____ even though it began to snow.
    A. playing   B. to play

_____ 4. We like _____ outside when the weather is warm and sunny.
    A. eating   B. to eat

_____ 5. We began _____ to the news when we heard the Olympics mentioned.
    A. listening   B. to listen

_____ 6. I was just beginning _____ asleep when the phone rang.
    A. falling   B. to fall

_____ 7. I really hate _____ late for appointments.
    A. being   B. to be

_____ 8. The cake was starting _____ when I took it out of the oven.
    A. burning   B. to burn

_____ 9. She's so impatient! She can't stand _____ in line for anything.
    A. waiting   B. to wait

_____ 10. I prefer _____ my bicycle to work because the automobile traffic is too heavy.
    A. riding   B. to ride

_____ 11. Lillian prefers _____ to taking the bus.
    A. walking   B. to walk

_____ 12. Tim prefers _____ than to jog for exercise.
    A. walking   B. to walk

_____ 13. The baby loves _____ in the car.
    A. riding   B. to ride

_____ 14. Near the end of the performance, the audience began _____ their feet on the floor.
    A. stamping   B. to stamp

_____ 15. The audience began to clap and _____ their feet on the floor.
    A. stamping   B. (to) stamp

_____ 16. The audience began clapping and _____ their feet on the floor.
    A. stamping   B. (to) stamp

_____ 17. My son sometimes forgets _____ the stove when he's finished cooking.
    A. turning off   B. to turn off

_____ 18. Alex will never forget _____ his first helicopter ride.
    A. taking   B. to take

_____ 19. Would you please remember _____ away all the tapes when you're finished listening to them?
    A. putting   B. to put

_____ 20. I remember _____ them away when I finished with them last night.
    A. putting   B. to put

_____ 21. I remember _____ Bolivia for the first time. It's a beautiful country.
    A. visiting   B. to visit

_____ 22. What am I going to do? I forgot _____ my calculus text, and I need it for the review today.
    A. bringing   B. to bring

_____ 23. My boss regrets _____ his secretary now that she is gone.
    A. firing   B. to fire

_____ 24. The letter said, "I regret _____ you that your application has been denied."
    A. informing   B. to inform

_____ 25. I haven't been able to get in touch with Shannon. I tried _____ her. Then I tried _____ her a letter. I tried _____ a message with her brother when I talked to him. Nothing worked.
    A. calling/writing/leaving   B. to call/to write/to leave

_____ 26. I always try _____ my bills on time, but sometimes I'm a little late.
    A. paying   B. to pay

◇ **PRACTICE 8—GUIDED STUDY: Gerund vs. infinitive. (Charts 4-3 → 4-6)**

Directions: Use the correct form of the verbs in parentheses and complete the sentence with your own words. Include a (PRO)NOUN OBJECT between the two verbs if necessary.

Examples:
    The fire marshal (_tell + unlock_) → _The fire marshal told us to unlock the back doors of the school to provide a fast exit in the event of an emergency._
    (. . .) (_be asked + lead_) → _Maria was asked to lead a group discussion in class yesterday._

1. Mr. (. . .) (_remind + finish_)
2. The teacher (_postpone + give_)
3. Students (_be required + have_)
4. The counselor (_advise + take_)
5. I (_try + learn_)
6. Ms. (. . .) (_warn + not open_)
7. I (_like + go + camp_)
8. (. . .) (_invite + go_)
9. (. . .) (_promise + not tell_)
10. We (_not be permitted + take_)
11. My friend (_ask + tell_)
12. When the wind (_begin + blow_)
13. I (_remember + call_)
14. (. . .) (_tell + wash_)
15. (. . .) (_be told + be_)
16. I (_avoid + get_)

Directions: Work with another person. One of you should read the beginning of the sentence, and the other, without looking at the book, should supply the correct response: ***to do it*** or ***doing it***. (If you are studying alone, cover up the answers in parentheses and check yourself as you go.)

Example: A: I enjoy....
*   B: ...doing it.*

1. I dislike . . . . (doing it)
2. She was ordered . . . . (to do it.)
3. I urged my friend . . . . (to do it.)
4. Can he afford . . . . (to do it?)
5. We all discussed . . . . (doing it.)
6. The institute requires us . . . . (to do it.)
7. We will eventually complete . . . . (doing it.)
8. The whole class practiced . . . . (doing it.)
9. I really don't care . . . . (to do it.)
10. Do you recommend . . . . (doing it?)
11. She was expected . . . . (to do it.)
12. Bill resented his roommate . . . . (doing it.)
13. Did the little boy admit . . . . (doing it?)
14. Please allow us . . . . (to do it.)
15. The whole family anticipated . . . . . . (doing it.)
16. No one recollected . . . . (doing it.)
17. Did you risk . . . . (doing it?)
18. Did they recall . . . . (doing it?)
19. My friend challenged me . . . . (to do it.)
20. Our director postponed . . . . (doing it.)
21. Do you mind . . . . (doing it?)
22. Why did he pretend . . . . (to do it?)
23. The teacher arranged . . . . (to do it.)
24. The regulations permit us . . . . (to do it.)
25. The dentist wanted to delay . . . . (doing it.)
26. Can anyone learn . . . . (to do it?)
27. Did someone offer . . . . (to do it?)
28. He doesn't deny . . . . (doing it.)
29. Somehow, the cat managed . . . . (to do it.)
30. Everyone avoided . . . . (doing it.)
31. The boy dared Al . . . . (to do it.)
32. Our teacher threatened . . . . (to do it.)
33. The contestant practiced . . . . (doing it.)
34. My friend consented . . . . (to do it.)
35. I miss . . . . (doing it.)

◇ PRACTICE 10—SELFSTUDY: Gerund vs. infinitive. (Charts 4-2 → 4-8)

Directions: Complete the sentences with the correct form, GERUND or INFINITIVE, using the words in parentheses.

1. The store offered _____ ***to refund*** _____ the money I paid for the book I returned. (*refund*)

2. Don't pretend ___**to be**___ what you aren't. (*be*)

3. I persuaded my brother-in-law not _____ that old car. (*buy*)

4. Annie denied _____ the brick through the window. (*throw*)

5. My father expects me _____ high marks in school. (*get*)

6. According to the sign on the restaurant door, all diners are required _____ shirts and shoes. (*wear*)

7. We are planning _____ several historical sites in Moscow. (*visit*)

8. There appears _____ no way to change our reservation for the play at this late date. (*be*)

9. For some strange reason, I keep _____ today is Saturday. (*think*)

10. All of the members agreed _____ the emergency meeting. (*attend*)

11. I've arranged _____ work early tomorrow. (*leave*)

12. Even though Anna had never cut anyone's hair before, she readily consented _____ her husband's hair. (*cut*)

13. Mary decided _____ her friend's critical remarks. (*ignore*)

14. My roommate says I have a terrible voice, so I stopped _____ in the shower. (*sing*)

15. Did the doctor mention _____ any foods in particular? (*avoid*)

16. The cashier always remembers _____ the money in her cash register each day before she leaves work. (*count*)

17. Let's hurry! We must finish _____ the office before 3:00 this afternoon. (*paint*)

18. The student with the highest average deserves _____ an "A". (*get*)

19. I appreciate your _____ for my dinner. I'll buy next time. (*pay*)

20. The physically handicapped child struggled _____ up with the other children on the playground, but she couldn't. (*keep*)

21. Janice misses _____ walks with her father in the evening now that she has moved away from home. (*take*)

22. The customs official demanded _____ what was inside the gift-wrapped box. (*know*)

23. We've discussed _____ to New York in the fall, but I'm worried about our children having to adjust to a new school system and new friends. (*move*)

24. Children shouldn't be allowed _____ violent programs on TV. (*watch*)

25. In a fit of anger, I ordered my neighbor _____ his mule off my property. (*keep*)

◇ PRACTICE 11—SELFSTUDY: Gerund vs. infinitive. (Charts 4-2 → 4-8)

Directions: Complete the sentences with the correct form, GERUND or INFINITIVE, using the words in parentheses.

1. The doctor was forced __***to operate***__ immediately to save the patient's life. (*operate*)

2. The newspaper hired Bill _____ pictures of the championship match between the two boxers. (*shoot*)

3. Most passengers dislike _____ to sit in small, uncomfortable seats on transoceanic flights. (*have*)

4. I chose _____ to Stanford University for my undergraduate studies. (*go*)

5. I must drive more carefully. I can't risk _____ another speeding ticket. (*get*)

6. All of the members agreed _____ the emergency meeting. (*attend*)

7. Jack promised _____ to the meeting. (*come*)

8. The sign warns you not _____ right on a red light. (*turn*)

9. Did Dick mean _____ Sue about the surprise party, or did it slip out accidentally? (*tell*)

10. You must keep _____ on the computer until you understand how to use all of the programs. (*practice*)

11. Our class volunteered _____ the classroom during the maintenance workers' strike. (*clean*)

12. When you get through _____ the newspaper, I could use your help in the kitchen. (*read*)

13. I think we should delay _____ these reports to the main office. (*send*)

14. The judge demanded _____ the original document, not the photocopy. (*see*)

15. After hearing the weather report, I advise you not _____ skiing this afternoon. (*go*)

16. George is interested in _____ an art class. (*take*)

17. I was furious. I threatened never _____ to him again. (*speak*)

18. My parents appreciated _____ the thank-you note you sent them. (*receive*)

19. The committee is planning _____ next Friday. (*meet*)

20. If I don't leave on the 15th, I will miss _____ home in time for my mother's birthday party. (*get*)

21. I know you're anxious to get out of here and get back home, but you should seriously consider _____ in the hospital a few more days. (*stay*)

22. Alex refused _____ for his rude behavior. (*apologize*)

23. When I was in the army, I had to swear _____ my senior officers' orders. (*obey*)

24. I don't recall _____ your dictionary anywhere in the apartment. Maybe you left it in the classroom. (*see*)

25. Mrs. Lind required the children _____ off their muddy boots before they came into the house. (*take*)

◇ PRACTICE 12—SELFSTUDY: Gerund vs. infinitive. (Charts 4-7 and 4-8)

Directions: Choose the correct answer.

___*A*___ 1. The groom anticipated _____ the wedding ceremony.
A. enjoying   B. to enjoy

_____ 2. The department store agreed _____ back the damaged radio.
A. taking   B. to take

_____ 3. Would the doctor mind _____ some time talking to me after the examination?
A. spending   B. to spend

_____ 4. We miss _____ Professor Sanders in Asian history this quarter.
A. having   B. to have

_____ 5. Dan failed _____ the firefighter's examination and was quite upset.
A. passing   B. to pass

_____ 6. The travelers anticipated _____ safely at their destination.
A. arriving   B. to arrive

_____ 7. She expects _____ her baby at the new hospital.
A. delivering   B. to deliver

_____ 8. The bad weather caused us _____ our connecting flight to Rome.
A. missing   B. to miss

_____ 9. We dislike _____ dinner at 9:00 P.M.
A. eating   B. to eat

_____ 10. Most of the students completed _____ their research papers on time.
A. writing   B. to write

_____ 11. My niece hopes _____ with me to Disneyland next April.
A. traveling   B. to travel

_____ 12. This note will remind me _____ the chicken for dinner tomorrow night.
        A. defrosting   B. to defrost

_____ 13. Willy denied _____ a whole bag of chocolate chip cookies before lunch.
        A. eating   B. to eat

_____ 14. You must swear _____ the truth in a court of law.
        A. telling   B. to tell

_____ 15. I didn't mean _____ him.
        A. interrupting   B. to interrupt

◇ PRACTICE 13—GUIDED STUDY: Gerund vs. infinitive. (Charts 4-7 and 4-8)

Directions: Make sentences from the following verb combinations. Select any tense for the first verb but use a GERUND or INFINITIVE for the second verb. Include a (PRO)NOUN OBJECT if necessary.

Examples:
    can't afford + buy → _I can't afford to buy a new car for at least another year._
    dare + dive → _My friends dared me to dive into the pool._

1. keep + play	14. not appreciate + hear
2. direct + save	15. fail + tell
3. regret + tell	16. resent + be
4. manage + get	17. resist + eat
5. remind + take	18. claim + know
6. be used to + stay	19. deserve + get
7. persuade + not buy	20. not recall + say
8. mention + give	21. look forward to + see
9. suggest + go	22. beg + give
10. can't imagine + travel	23. agree + hire + work
11. recommend + take	24. remember + tell + be
12. convince + go + swim	25. urge + practice + speak
13. miss + be	26. tell + keep + try + call

◇ PRACTICE 14—GUIDED STUDY: Using gerunds as subjects. (Chart 4-10)

Directions: Using your own words, complete the sentences using GERUND phrases as subjects.

Examples:
    . . . isn't easy. → _Climbing to the top of a mountain isn't easy._
    . . . is a demanding job. → _Managing a major corporation is a demanding job._

1. . . . wears me out.	7. . . . demands patience and a sense of humor.
2. . . . can be difficult.	8. . . . is a complicated process.
3. . . . turned out to be a mistake.	9. . . . is very frustrating.
4. . . . will only add to your problems.	10. . . . was a real disappointment.
5. . . . has changed my life.	11. . . . looks easy.
6. . . . requires great skill and concentration.	12. . . . never works.

◇ PRACTICE 15.   GUIDED STUDY: Using *it* + infinitive. (Chart 4-9)

Directions: Make sentences beginning with **it**. Use a form of the given expression in your sentence, followed by an INFINITIVE phrase.

Examples:
   be dangerous → *It's dangerous to ride a motorcycle without wearing a helmet.*
   be difficult → *It was difficult for me to quit my job and go back to school.*

1. be important
2. be boring
3. not be easy
4. be foolish
5. must be interesting

6. be always a pleasure
7. be clever of you
8. not cost much money
9. be necessary
10. might be a good idea

◇ PRACTICE 16—SELFSTUDY: (*In order*) *to.* (Chart 4-10)

Directions: Add *in order* wherever possible. If nothing should be added, write the Ø.

1. I went to the garden center _____*in order*_____ to get some fertilizer for my flowers.

2. When the teacher asked him a question, Jack pretended _____Ø_____ to understand what she was saying.

3. My roommate asked me _____ to repair the leaky faucet.

4. I bought a new screwdriver _____ to repair my bicycle.

5. Emily likes _____ to go ice skating every weekend.

6. Please open the door _____ to let some fresh air in.

7. My mother always said I should eat lots of green vegetables _____ to make my body strong.

8. John climbed onto a chair _____ to change a light bulb in the ceiling.

9. I really want _____ to learn Italian before I visit Venice next year.

10. Elizabeth has to practice at least four hours every day _____ to be ready for her piano recital next month.

11. I jog three times a week _____ to stay healthy.

12. It is a good idea _____ to know where your children are at all times.

13. Jim finally went to the dentist _____ to get some relief from his toothache.

14. I need to find her _____ to talk to her.

15. Claudia has to work at two jobs _____ to support herself and her three children.

16. It's easier for me _____ to understand written English than spoken English.

17. The students were practicing speaking English into a tape recorder _____ to improve their pronunciation.

18. It isn't important _____ to speak English without any accent at all as long as people understand what you're saying.

◇ PRACTICE 17—GUIDED STUDY: Adjectives followed by infinitives. (Chart 4-11)

Directions: Complete the sentences with the expressions in the list and with your own words. Use INFINITIVE phrases in your completions. Use any expression in the list that is appropriate, and use it more than once if you wish.

ashamed to	*delighted to*	*fortunate to*	*ready to*
careful to	*determined to*	*likely to*	*reluctant to*
certain to	*eager to*	*not prepared to*	*willing to*

1. Mary always speeds on the expressway. She's . . . .
   → *She's certain to get stopped by the police.* OR:
   → *She's likely to get a ticket.*
2. There have been a lot of burglaries in my neighborhood recently, so I have started taking precautions. Now I am always very . . . .
3. I've worked hard all day long. Enough's enough. I'm . . . .
4. Next month, I'm going to a family reunion—the first one in 25 years. I'm very much looking forward to it. I'm . . . .
5. Some children grow up in unhappy homes. My family, however, has always been loving and supportive. I'm . . . .
6. Joe's run out of money again, but he doesn't want anyone to know his situation. He needs money desperately, but he's . . . .
7. Rosalyn wants to become an astronaut. That has been her dream since she was a little girl. She has been working hard toward her goal and is . . . .
8. Peter was offered an excellent job in another state, but his wife and children don't want to move. He's not sure what to do. Although he would like the job, he's . . . .
9. At the street market, I bartered with the seller over the price of the garment. He wanted $20. I offered $10. In the end, he was . . . .
10. Jason is going fishing today. He's . . . .
11. Our neighbors had extra tickets to the ballet, so they invited us to go with them. Since both of us love the ballet, we were . . . .
12. It takes maturity and understanding to make wise decisions. Thomas is only seventeen years old. He's . . . .

◇ PRACTICE 18—SELFSTUDY: *Too* vs. *very.* (Chart 4-12)

Directions: Add *too* or *very* to the sentences, as appropriate.

1. The box is __*very*__ heavy, but I can lift it.
2. John dropped his physics course because it was __*too*__ difficult for him.
3. I think it's _____ late to get tickets to the concert. I heard they were all sold.
4. It's _____ cold today, but I'm still going to take my daily walk.

5. Our cat is fourteen years old. Now he's _____ old to catch mice in the field across the street.

6. It's _____ dark to see in here. Please turn on the lights.

7. She was _____ ill. Nevertheless, she came to the family reunion.

8. The boys were _____ busy to help me clean out the garage, so I did it myself.

9. Learning a second language is _____ difficult, but most of the students are doing well.

10. We enjoyed our dinner at that restaurant last night. It was _____ good.

11. Professor Andrews is always _____ interesting, but I'm _____ tired to go to the lecture tonight.

12. He's _____ young to understand. He'll understand when he's older.

13. The meal was _____ good. I enjoyed every morsel.

14. I'm _____ sleepy to watch the rest of the TV movie. Let me know how it turns out.

15. Sally was running _____ fast for me to keep up with her, so I lagged behind.

◇ **PRACTICE 19—SELFSTUDY: Passive infinitives. (Chart 4-13)**

Directions: Choose the correct answer.

_____ 1. When I told Tim the news, he seemed _____.
  A. to surprise   B. to be surprised

_____ 2. Ms. Thompson is always willing to help, but she doesn't want _____ at home unless there is an emergency.
  A. to call   B. to be called

_____ 3. The children agreed _____ the candy equally.
  A. to divide   B. to be divided

_____ 4. Janice is going to fill out an application. She wants _____ for the job.
  A. to consider   B. to be considered

_____ 5. I expected _____ to the party, but I wasn't.
  A. to invite   B. to be invited

_____ 6. The mail is supposed _____ at noon.
  A. to deliver   B. to be delivered

_____ 7. I expect _____ at the airport by my uncle.
  A. to meet   B. to be met

_____ 8. Mr. Steinberg offered _____ us to the train station.
  A. to drive   B. to be driven

_____ 9. The children appear _____ about the trip.
  A. to excite   B. to be excited

_____ 10. Your compositions are supposed _____ in ink.
  A. to write   B. to be written

◇ PRACTICE 20—SELFSTUDY: Passive gerunds. (Chart 4-13)

Directions: Choose the correct answer.

_____   1. I don't appreciate _____ when I'm speaking.
          A. interrupting   B. being interrupted

_____   2. Avoid _____ your houseplants too much water.
          A. giving   B. being given

_____   3. The mountain climbers are in danger of _____ by an avalanche.
          A. killing   B. being killed

_____   4. Does Dr. Johnson mind _____ at home if his patients need his help?
          A. calling   B. being called

_____   5. I'm interested in _____ my communication skills.
          A. improving   B. being improved

_____   6. Mrs. Gates appreciated _____ breakfast in bed when she wasn't feeling well.
          A. serving   B. being served

_____   7. Jack Welles has a good chance of _____. I know I'm going to vote for him.
          A. electing   B. being elected

_____   8. Sally's low test scores kept her from _____ to the university.
          A. admitting   B. being admitted

_____   9. Mr. Miller gave no indication of _____ his mind.
          A. changing   B. being changed

_____ 10. Sometimes adolescents complain about not _____ by their parents.
          A. understanding   B. being understood

◇ PRACTICE 21—SELFSTUDY: Passive infinitives and gerunds. (Chart 4-13)

Directions: Choose the correct answer.

_____   1. Instead of _____ about the good news, Tom seemed to be indifferent.
          A. exciting   B. being excited   C. to excite   D. to be excited

_____   2. The new students hope _____ in many of the school's social activities.
          A. including   B. being included   C. to include   D. to be included

_____   3. The owner of the building supply store doesn't mind _____ his customers discounts
          when they buy in large quantities.
          A. giving   B. being given   C. to give   D. to be given

_____   4. Jack got into trouble when he refused _____ his briefcase for the customs officer.
          A. opening   B. being opened   C. to open   D. to be opened

_____   5. Barbara didn't mention _____ about her progress report at work, but I'm sure she is.
          A. concerning   B. being concerned
          C. to concern   D. to be concerned

_____   6. The City Parks Department is putting in several miles of new trails because so many
          people have said that they enjoy _____ on them.
          A. walking   B. being walked   C. to walk   D. to be walked

_____ 7. You'd better save some money for a rainy day. You can't count on _____ by your parents every time you get into financial difficulty.
    A. rescuing   B. being rescued   C. to rescue   D. to be rescued

_____ 8. Please forgive me. I didn't mean _____ you.
    A. upsetting   B. being upset   C. to upset   D. to be upset

_____ 9. I don't remember _____ of the decision to change the company policy on vacations. When was it decided?
    A. telling   B. being told   C. to tell   D. to be told

_____ 10. Ms. Drake expects _____ about any revisions in her manuscript before it is printed.
    A. consulting   B. being consulted
    C. to consult   D. to be consulted

_____ 11. Sally gave such a good speech that I couldn't resist _____ loudly when she finished.
    A. applauding   B. being applauded
    C. to applaud   D. to be applauded

_____ 12. Tommy admitted _____ the rock through the window.
    A. throwing   B. being thrown   C. to throw   D. to be thrown

_____ 13. If you want to develop inner tranquility, you have to stop _____ by every little thing that happens.
    A. bothering   B. being bothered
    C. to bother   D. to be bothered

_____ 14. Paul really didn't mind _____ by the party to celebrate his fortieth birthday, although he told his friends that they shouldn't have done it.
    A. surprising   B. being surprised
    C. to surprise   D. to be surprised

_____ 15. Anne hoped _____ to join the private club. She could make important business contacts there.
    A. inviting   B. being invited   C. to invite   D. to be invited

◇ **PRACTICE 22—SELFSTUDY: Past and past-passive infinitives and gerunds. (Chart 4-13)**

Directions: Choose the correct answer.

_____ 1. Are you sure you told me? I don't recall _____ about it.
    A. having told   B. having been told
    C. to have told   D. to have been told

_____ 2. Dan appears _____ some weight. Has he been ill?
    A. having lost   B. having been lost
    C. to have lost   D. to have been lost

_____ 3. Tom made a bad mistake at work, but his boss didn't fire him. He's lucky _____ a second chance.
    A. having given   B. having been given
    C. to have given   D. to have been given

_____ 4. Dr. Wilson is a brilliant and dedicated scientist who had expected to be selected as the director of the institute. She was very surprised not _____ the position.
    A. having offered   B. having been offered
    C. to have offered   D. to have been offered

_____ 5. By the time their baby arrives, the Johnsons hope _____ painting and decorating the new nursery.
    A. having finished   B. having been finished
    C. to have finished   D. to have been finished

_____ 6. We would like _____ to the president's reception, but we weren't.
   A. having invited   B. having been invited
   C. to have invited   D. to have been invited

_____ 7. The stockbroker denied _____ of the secret business deal.
   A. having informed   B. having been informed
   C. to have informed   D. to have been informed

_____ 8. George mentioned _____ in an accident as a child, but he never told us the details.
   A. having injured   B. having been injured
   C. to have injured   D. to have been injured

_____ 9. The Smiths wanted to give their son every advantage. However, they now regret
         _____ him by providing too many material possessions.
   A. having spoiled   B. having been spoiled
   C. to have spoiled   D. to have been spoiled

_____ 10. The spy admitted _____ some highly secret information to enemy agents.
   A. having given   B. having been given
   C. to have given   D. to have been given

◇ PRACTICE 23—SELFSTUDY: Using a possessive to modify a gerund. (Chart 4-15)

Directions: Combine the following. Change "that fact" to a GERUND phrase. Use formal English.

Example:
   We answered all of the exam questions correctly. The teacher was pleased with that fact.
   → *The teacher was pleased with our answering* (OR: *having answered*) *all of the exam questions correctly.*

1. I lost my new watch. My mother was angry about that fact.

2. They are going to spend their vacation with us. We look forward to that fact.

3. Tony failed the economics test even though he studied hard. No one can understand that fact.

4. The students are required to pay an extra fee to use the laboratory. I am upset about that fact.

5. Mary worked late to finish the project. The supervisor appreciated that fact.

6. You are late to work every morning. I will no longer tolerate that fact.

◇ PRACTICE 24—SELFSTUDY: Gerunds and infinitives. (Charts 4-1 → 4-15)

Directions: Choose the correct answer.

_____ 1. Alice didn't expect _____ to Bill's party.
   A. asking   B. being asked   C. to ask   D. to be asked

_____ 2. I finally finished _____ at 7:00 P.M. and served dinner.
   A. cooking   B. being cooked   C. to cook   D. to be cooked

_____ 3. Sam always remembers _____ in the garage so that the driveway is free for other cars.
   A. parking   B. being parked   C. to park   D. to be parked

_____ 4. The nurse suggested _____ two aspirin.
   A. taking   B. being taken   C. to take   D. to be taken

_____ 5. Would you mind not _____ the radio until I've finished with this phone call?
   A. turning on   B. being turned on
   C. to turn on   D. to be turned on

_____ 6. They were fortunate _____ from the fire before the building collapsed.
   A. rescuing
   B. to have rescued
   C. to rescue
   D. to have been rescued

_____ 7. The mouse family avoided _____ by coming out only when the house was empty and the two cats were outside.
   A. catching
   B. being caught
   C. to have been caught
   D. to be caught

_____ 8. The baby continued _____ even after she was picked up.
   A. being crying
   B. having cried
   C. to cry
   D. having been crying

_____ 9. Arthur pretended not _____ hurt when his younger sister bit him.
   A. having   B. be   C. to have   D. to have been

_____ 10. We were shocked to hear the news of your _____.
   A. having fired
   B. having been fired
   C. to be fired
   D. to have been fired

_____ 11. Even though she was much younger than the other children, Alexis demanded _____ in the game they were playing.
   A. including   B. being included   C. to include   D. to be included

_____ 12. Our mechanic said that he expects _____ the brakes on the car before we pick it up.
   A. fixing
   B. being fixed
   C. to have fixed
   D. to have been fixed

_____ 13. Marge's children are used to _____ after school every day. They don't have to walk home.
   A. picking up
   B. being picked up
   C. be picked up
   D. pick up

_____ 14. The bus driver was so tired of _____ the same route every day that he asked for a transfer.
   A. to drive   B. being driven   C. driving   D. drive

_____ 15. I'm sure it's not my fault that Peter found out what we were planning. I don't remember _____ anyone about it.
   A. having told   B. being told   C. to tell   D. to be told

◇ **PRACTICE 25—GUIDED STUDY:** Gerunds and infinitives. (Charts 4-1 → 4-15)

Directions: Complete the sentences. Each sentence should contain a GERUND or INFINITIVE.

Example: You are required . . . .
  → *You are required to stop at the border when entering another country.*

1. Your not wanting . . . .
2. It's important for . . . .
3. I'll never forget . . . .
4. Jack advised not . . . .
5. I'm not willing . . . .
6. My apartment needs . . . .
7. . . . enough energy . . . .
8. . . . in order to save . . . .
9. . . . to be told about . . . .
10. . . . had just begun . . . when . . . .
11. Do you think it is easy . . . .
12. . . . my having been . . . .
13. Have you ever considered . . .
14. . . . is likely . . . .
15. Most people object . . . .
16. . . . try to avoid . . . .

◇ **PRACTICE 26—SELFSTUDY:** Using verbs of perception. (Chart 4-16)

Directions: Complete the sentences with the words in the list. Use each word only one time. Use the SIMPLE form or the *-ing* form, whichever seems better to you.

arrive	*emerge*	*open*	*prevent*
chirp	*explain*	*perform*	*snore*
climb	*melt*	✔ *practice*	*win*

1. Whenever I have free time, I like to watch the basketball team ____*practice*____.

2. When I heard the front door _____, I got up to see if someone had come in.

3. A few years ago, I saw a dog _____ a child from wandering into a busy street by standing in front of her and not letting her get by.

4. It was a thrill to see my brother _____ the chess tournament last year.

5. Uncle Jake is in his bedroom right now. I can hear him _____.

6. I was amazed to see the firefighters _____ so soon after my call.

7. The boy watched the butterfly _____ from its cocoon.

8. It is educational for children to observe adults _____ their daily tasks.

9. When I look at my gym teacher _____ the rope, it looks easy, but when I try it, it is hard.

10. Hearing the birds _____ tells us that spring has indeed arrived.

11. I listened to the teacher _____ how to solve the math problem.

12. I held out my hand and watched each snowflake _____ as soon as it touched my skin.

◇ PRACTICE 27—GUIDED STUDY: Using verbs of perception. (Chart 4-16)

Directions: Make sentences from the given verb combinations. Use the **-ing** form for the second verb if appropriate.

Examples:
    hear + shout at → *At work yesterday, I heard someone shouting at Mr. Lewis in the next room.*
    listen to + speak → *Lionel has a wonderful British accent. I enjoy listening to him speak.*

1. hear + ring
2. see + hit
3. watch + take
4. look at + sail
5. observe + march

6. see + sink
7. listen to + howl
8. watch + do
9. see + put
10. watch + throw

◇ PRACTICE 28—SELFSTUDY: *Let, help*, and causative verbs. (Charts 4-17 and 4-18)

Directions: Choose the correct answer(s).

__*C*__   1. Instead of buying a new pair of shoes, I had my old ones _____.
          A. repair   B. to repair   C. repaired

_*A, B*_ 2. I helped my daughter _____ her homework.
          A. finish   B. to finish   C. finished

_____   3. I made my son _____ the windows before he could go outside to play with his friends.
          A. wash   B. to wash   C. washed

_____   4. Maria had her landlord _____ the broken window before winter.
          A. fix   B. to fix   C. fixed

_____   5. To please my daughter, I had her old bicycle _____ bright red.
          A. paint   B. to paint   C. painted

_____   6. Sam was reluctant, but we finally got him _____ his guitar for us.
          A. play   B. to play   C. played

_____   7. When I had to make an emergency phone call, the secretary let me _____ her phone.
          A. use   B. to use   C. used

_____   8. Jack, could you help me _____ a place in the garden to plant some tomatoes?
          A. dig   B. to dig   C. dug

_____ 9. Before we leave, let's have Shelley _____ a map for us so we won't get lost.

          A. draw   B. to draw   C. drawn

_____ 10. Are you going to let me _____ that last piece of blueberry pie?

          A. eat   B. to eat   C. eaten

◇ PRACTICE 29—GUIDED STUDY: *Let, help,* and causative verbs. (Charts 4-17 and 4-18)

Directions: Make sentences from the given combinations.

Examples:

    let *(someone)* + play → *When I was a child, my older brother wouldn't let me play with him and his friends.*
    get *(someone)* + help → *I got my roommate to help me prepare for my final exam in physics.*
    have *(something)* + repaired → *I had the brakes on my car repaired at Morgan's Garage.*

1. let *(someone)* + cook
2. make *(someone)* + sit
3. get *(someone)* + buy
4. have *(something)* + filled
5. have *(someone)* + bring

6. help *(someone)* + feed
7. let *(someone)* + show
8. make *(someone)* + stop
9. get *(something)* + closed
10. have *(someone)* + find out

◇ PRACTICE 30—GUIDED STUDY: Special expressions followed by the *-ing* form of a verb. (Chart 4-19)

Directions: Make sentences from the given combinations.

Examples:

    have a difficult time + understand → *I have a difficult time understanding the teacher's explanations in calculus.*
    spend *(time)* + polish → *The soldier spent an hour polishing his boots.*

1. have trouble + remember
2. stand *(place)* + wait
3. have a hard time + learn
4. sit *(place)* + think
5. have a good time + play
6. lie *(place)* + dream

7. have difficulty + say
8. have fun + sing and dance
9. find *(someone)* + study
10. spend *(time)* + chat
11. waste *(money)* + try
12. catch *(someone)* + take

◇ PRACTICE 31—SELFSTUDY: Verb form review. (Charts 4-1 → 4-19)

Directions: Choose the correct answer.

_____ 1. I enjoy _____ to the park on summer evenings.

          A. to go   B. going   C. being gone   D. go

_____ 2. Don't forget _____ home as soon as you arrive at your destination.

          A. to call   B. calling   C. having called   D. to be called

_____ 3. When I kept getting unwanted calls, I called the phone company and had my phone number _____. The process was easier than I expected it to be.

          A. change   B. changed   C. to change   D. changing

_____ 4. Jean should seriously consider _____ an actress. She is a very talented performer.

          A. to become   B. become   C. becoming   D. will become

_____ 5. _____ television to the exclusion of all other activities is not a healthy habit for a growing child.

A. To be watched   B. Being watched   C. Watching   D. Watch

_____ 6. After their children had grown up, Mr. and Mrs. Sills decided _____ to a condominium in the city. They've never been sorry.

A. to have moved   B. moving   C. move   D. to move

_____ 7. I truly appreciated _____ to give the commencement address, but I wasn't able to accept the honor because of a previous commitment.

A. asking   B. to have asked
C. to ask   D. having been asked

_____ 8. The store manager caught the cashier _____ money from the cash register and promptly called the police. They discovered that it had been going on for a long time.

A. to sneak   B. sneaking
C. to have sneaked   D. being sneaked

_____ 9. My roommate's handwriting is very bad, so he had me _____ his paper for him last night.

A. to type   B. type   C. to have typed   D. typed

_____ 10. The municipal authorities advised _____ all drinking water during the emergency.

A. to boil   B. to be boiled   C. boiling   D. boil

_____ 11. If we leave now for our trip, we can drive half the distance before we stop _____ lunch.

A. having   B. to have   C. having had   D. for having

_____ 12. Out schedule is not working out. We should discuss _____ our daily routine. I don't feel as though we're getting enough accomplished.

A. changing   B. to change
C. to have changed   D. being changed

_____ 13. I can't recall _____ that old movie, but maybe I did many years ago.

A. having seen   B. to have seen
C. to see   D. having been seen

_____ 14. Our school basketball team won the championship game by _____ two points in the last five seconds. It was the most exciting game I have ever attended.

A. being scored   B. to score   C. scoring   D. score

_____ 15. The flight attendants made all the passengers _____ their seat belts during the turbulence.

A. to buckle   B. to have buckled
C. buckling   D. buckle

_____ 16. It has become necessary _____ water in the metropolitan area because of the severe drought.

A. rationing   B. ration
C. to have rationed   D. to ration

_____ 17. You can't blame Ralph for _____ to eat that dessert. It looked delicious.

A. to be tempted   B. tempted
C. be tempted   D. having been tempted

_____ 18. Let's leave early, so we'll be ahead of the rush of commuters. We can't risk _____ in heavy traffic during rush hour.

A. holding up   B. being held up
C. having held up   D. to hold up

_____ 19. It is always interesting _____ people in airports while you're waiting for a flight.
   A. being observed   B. observe
   C. to have observed   D. to observe

_____ 20. I got everyone in the family _____ Jane's birthday card before I sent it to her.
   A. sign   B. signed   C. to sign   D. having signed

◇ **PRACTICE 32—SELFSTUDY: Verb form review (Charts 4-1 → 4-19)**

Directions: Complete the sentence with an appropriate form of the verb in parentheses.

1. Bill decided (*buy*) __*to buy*__ a new car rather than a used one.

2. We delayed (*open*) _____ the doors of the examination room until exactly 9:00.

3. I really dislike (*ask*) _____ to answer questions in class when I haven't prepared my lesson.

4. I certainly didn't anticipate (*have*) _____ to wait in line for three hours for tickets to the baseball game!

5. When I was younger, I used (*wear*) _____ mini-skirts and bright colors. Now I am accustomed to (*dress*) _____ more conservatively.

6. My children enjoy (*allow*) _____ to stay up late when there's something special on TV.

7. Skydivers must have nerves of steel. I can't imagine (*jump*) _____ out of a plane and (*fall*) _____ to the earth. What if the parachute didn't open?

8. We are looking forward to (*take*) _____ on a tour of Athens by our Greek friends.

9. (*Observe*) _____ the sun (*climb*) _____ above the horizon at dawn makes one (*realize*) _____ the earth is indeed turning.

10. I told the mail carrier that we would be away for two weeks on vacation. I asked her (*stop*) _____ (*deliver*) _____ our mail until the 21st. She told me (*fill*) _____ out a form at the post office so that the post office would hold our mail until we returned.

11. The elderly man next door is just sitting in his rocking chair (*gaze*) _____ out the window. I wish there were something I could do (*cheer*) _____ him up.

12. I don't understand how you got the wrong results. When I look over your notes, your chemistry experiment seems (*perform*) _____ correctly. But something is wrong somewhere.

13. My mother always made me (*wash*) _____ my hands before every meal. She wouldn't let me (*come*) _____ to the dinner table until she had inspected my hands.

14. I resent (*have*) _____ to work on this project with Fred. I know I'll end up with most of the work falling on my shoulders.

15. John admitted (*surprise*) _____ by the unexpected birthday party last night. We had a lot of fun (*plan*) _____ it.

16. Rick moved from a big city to a small town. He appreciates (*be*) _____ able to drive to work in five minutes with very little traffic congestion.

17. The power lines outside my house were dangerous. I finally got the power company (*move*) _____ them to a safer place.

18. I wanted (*help*) _____ them (*resolve*) _____ their differences, but Sally persuaded me (*interfere, not*) _____.

19. The witness to the murder asked not (*identify*) _____ in the newspaper. She wanted her name kept secret.

20. Sara was encouraged by her teachers (*apply*) _____ for study at the Art Institute.

21. I was happy (*learn*) _____ of your new position in the company, but I was disappointed (*discover*) _____ that you had recommended (*promote*) _____ Carl to your old position instead of me.

22. I don't mind (*remind*) _____ you every day (*lock*) _____ the door when you leave the apartment, but I would appreciate your (*try*) _____ (*remember*) _____ on your own.

23. It is generally considered impolite (*pick*) _____ your teeth at the dinner table.

24. I don't recall (*meet*) _____ Mr. Parker before. I'm sure I haven't. I'd like (*introduce*) _____ to him. Would you do the honors?

25. Now I remember your (*ask*) _____ me to bring sandwiches to the picnic. Your complaints about my (*forget*) _____ things seem justified. I'm sorry.

26. Ed's boss recommended him for the job. Ed was pleased (*consider*) _____ _____ for the job even though he didn't get it.

27. After our automobile accident, the insurance company had a stack of papers for us to sign, but our lawyer advised us (*sign, not*) _____ them until she had a chance to study them very carefully.

28. I wasn't tired enough (*sleep*) _____ last night. For a long time, I just lay in bed (*think*) _____ about my career and my future.

29. John was responsible for (*notify*) _____ everyone about the meeting, but he apparently failed (*call*) _____ several people. As a result, not enough people showed up, and we have to try to get everybody together again soon.

30. Art smelled something (*burn*) _____. When he ran into the kitchen, he saw fire (*come*) _____ out of the oven and panicked. If Barbara hadn't come running in with the fire extinguisher, I don't know what would have happened.

◇ PRACTICE 33—GUIDED STUDY: Verb form review. (Charts 4-1 → 4-19)

Directions: Complete the sentence with the appropriate form of the verb in parentheses.

1. After I decided (*have*) _____ a garage (*build*) _____ next to the house, I hired a carpenter (*do*) _____ the work.

2. The coach didn't let anyone (*watch*) _____ the team (*practice*) _____ before the championship game. He wanted to keep the opposing team from (*find*) _____ out about the new plays he had devised.

3. Jeff applied to medical school many months ago. Now he's so concerned about (accept)

_____ into medical school that he's having a difficult time

(concentrate) _____ on the courses he's taking this term.

4. My son is playing in his first piano recital this evening. I'm looking forward to (hear)

_____ him (play) _____, but I know he's worried about (forget)

_____ the right notes and (make) _____ a fool of himself. I

told him just (relax) _____ and (enjoy) _____ himself.

5. It may be impossible (persuade) _____ my mother (give) _____

up her job even though she's having health problems. We can't even get her (cut)

_____ down on her working hours. She enjoys (work) _____ so much

that she refuses (retire) _____ and (take) _____ it easy. I admire her

for (dedicate) _____ to her work, but I also want her to take

care of her health.

6. There's not much point in (waste) _____ a lot of time and energy on that project.

It's likely (fail) _____ no matter what we do. Spend your time (do) _____

something more worthwhile.

7. Traffic has become too heavy for the Steinbergs (commute) _____ easily to

their jobs in the city. They're considering (move) _____ to an apartment close to

their places of work. They don't want (give) _____ up their present home in the

suburbs, but they need (live) _____ in the city and (be) _____ closer

to their work so they can spend more time (do) _____ the things they really enjoy (do)

_____ in their free time.

8. Last week I was sick with the flu. It made me (feel) _____ awful. I didn't have

enough energy (get) _____ out of bed. I just lay there (feel) _____

sorry for myself. When my father heard me (sneeze) _____ and (cough)

_____, he opened my bedroom door (ask) _____ me if I needed

anything. I was really happy (see) _____ his kind and caring face, but there wasn't

anything he could do to make the flu (go) _____ away.

9. Fish don't use their teeth for (chew) _____. They use them for (grab)

_____, (hold) _____, or (tear) _____. Most fish

(swallow) _____ their prey whole.

10. (Attend) _____ the dance proved to be an (embarrass) _____

experience for me, especially since I don't know how to dance. I felt like a fish out of water. I

wanted (hide) _____ someplace or (get) _____ out of there, but my

friend wouldn't let me (leave) _____.

11. I'm over sixty now, but I enjoy (recall) _____ my high-school days. I

remember (choose) _____ by my classmates as "Most Likely to

Succeed'' when I was a senior. My best friend was chosen as "Least Likely to Succeed," and he is now the president of an electronics company. Once in a while when we get together, we have a good time (*look*) _____ through the high-school yearbook and (*laugh*) _____ at the way we looked then. We reminisce about (*act*) _____ in school dramas and (*play*) _____ on the basketball team. We remember (*be*) _____ serious young men who knew how to have fun. We congratulate ourselves for (*achieve*) _____ more than we had thought we could when we were eighteen.

12. I can't seem (*get*) _____ rid of the cockroaches in my apartment. I see them (*run*) _____ all over my kitchen counters every night. It drives me crazy. I'm considering (*have*) _____ the whole apartment (*spray*) _____ by a professional pest control expert.

13. The employees were unhappy when the new management took over. They weren't accustomed to (*treat*) _____ disrespectfully by the managers of the production departments. By (*threaten*) _____ (*stop*) _____ (*work*) _____, they got the company (*listen*) _____ to their grievances. In the end, a strike was averted.

14. Our house needs (*clean*) _____. The floors need (*sweep*) _____. The dishes need (*wash*) _____. The furniture needs (*dust*) _____. However, I think I'll read a book. (*Read*) _____ is a lot more interesting than (*do*) _____ housework.

15. According to some estimates, well over half of the world's population is functionally illiterate. Imagine (*be*) _____ a parent with a sick child and (*be*) _____ unable to read the directions on a medicine bottle. We all know that it is important for medical directions (*understand*) _____ clearly. Many medical professionals are working today (*bridge*) _____ the literacy gap by (*teach*) _____ health care through pictures.

16. As an adult, I very much appreciate (*give*) _____ the opportunity to travel extensively with my parents when I was a child. Those experiences were important in (*form*) _____ my view of the world. I learned (*accept*) _____ different customs and beliefs. At times, I would resist (*go*) _____ away on another trip, especially when I was a teenager. In the end, I always accompanied my parents, and I am grateful that I did. I didn't understand at that time how those trips would influence my later life. My (*be*) _____ a compassionate and caring adult is due in large part to my (*expose*) _____ to many different ways of life as a child.

17. (*Find*) _____ a cure for the common cold does not appear (*be*) _____ imminent. Colds are caused by hundreds of different viruses. You can possibly avoid (*expose*)

_____ to the viruses by (*stay*) _____ away from those with colds, but it's almost impossible (*avoid*) _____ the viruses completely. If you want (*minimize*) _____ the risk of (*get*) _____ a cold, it is prudent (*get*) _____ enough rest and (*eat*) _____ properly. Some people believe in (*take*) _____ large amounts of Vitamin C. In the long run, it is probably easier (*prevent*) _____ (*catch*) _____ a cold than it is to cure one.

18. Modern cars have systems that protect us from (*inconvenience*) _____ _____ or (*hurt*) _____ by our own carelessness. In most cars, when the keys are left in the ignition, a buzz sounds in order (*remind*) _____ the driver (*remove*) _____ them. In some models, if the driver does not remember (*turn*) _____ off the lights, it does not matter because the lights go off automatically. In some cases, when the seat belts are not buckled, the ignition does not start and then the driver is actually forced (*buckle*) _____ up. Often when the driver has failed (*shut*) _____ a door properly, another signal noise may be given. A few cars emit sounds to warn us (*fill*) _____ the tank before it is completely empty.

   It is easy (*forget*) _____ (*do*) _____ many routine tasks in (*drive*) _____ a car. The automatic warning systems help drivers (*avoid*) _____ (*make*) _____ some common mistakes. While some people may resent (*instruct*) _____ by their own automobiles (*perform*) _____ certain procedures, many others do not mind at all (*remind*) _____ (*carry*) _____ out these easily overlooked procedures.

◇ PRACTICE 34—SELFSTUDY: Error analysis. (Chapter 4)

Directions: Correct the errors in the following sentences.

1. Please promise not telling anybody my secret.
2. I would appreciate having heard from you soon.
3. Parents should never let very young children to stay at home alone.
4. Maria has never complained about have a handicap.
5. Mr. Lee didn't remember bring his passport when he went to the consulate.
6. Lillian deserves to be tell the truth about what happened last night.
7. Ali no speak Spanish, and Juan not know Arabic. But they communicate well by speak English when they be together.

8. I enjoyed to talk to her on the phone. I look forward to see her next week.

9. During a fire drill, everyone is required leaving the building.

10. Attend the premiere of the new musical play was a big thrill for me.

11. Don't keep to be asking me the same questions over and over.

12. I anticipate to arrive at the airport about 3:00 P.M.

13. Let me to help you carrying that table upstairs.

14. When I entered the room, I found my young son stand on the kitchen table.

◇ **PRACTICE 35—GUIDED STUDY: Verb forms.**

Directions: Write a composition for me, your reader, in which you explain exactly how to do something. Choose any topic that you know well. Assume that I know almost nothing about your topic. I have not had the experiences you have had. I don't know what you know. You must teach me. In your composition, use the words "I" and "you". Explain why/how you know about this topic. Address your information directly to your reader.
    Possible topics follow.

How to:	buy a used car	prepare a meal
	travel to a particular place	write a story
	open a bank account	paint a room
	get a job	repair a car
	take care of someone who has the flu	design a bridge
	plant a garden	study a language
	rent an apartment	organize a meeting
	register at a hotel	decorate a home
	breed dairy cows	teach a class
	interpret an X-ray	maintain a farm
	change a flat tire	start a business
	play a guitar	live abroad
	catch a fish	play a game

Example of an introductory paragraph:

Have you ever thought about buying a used car? When I was in my late teens, I decided I had to have a car. I worked hard and saved my money. When the time came, I convinced my best friend to accompany me to a used car lot. I didn't really know what I was doing, so I knew I needed him to help me. When we got to the lot, the salesman had us look at lots of cars. Suddenly we came upon the car of my dreams: a small, black sports convertible. It was classy, comfortable, shiny, and had leather seats, not to mention a powerful engine and lots of speed. My friend urged me to think it over, but I was so excited I handed the salesman my check for the first of many payments. Of course, I had no idea that the car was simply a beautiful pile of junk. I learned that later when everything started to go wrong with it. I'm older and wiser now, and even though I'm not a connoisseur of automobiles, I'd like to share my experiences with you and discuss what you should consider before you buy a used car.

Directions: Choose the correct answer.

Example:

___C___   *The office staff decided _____ a retirement party for Dolores.*
      A. *having had*   B. *to have had*   C. *to have*   D. *having*

_____ 1. I don't blame you for not _____ outside in this awful weather.
      A. wanting to go   B. wanting go   C. want to go   D. to want go

_____ 2. I think I hear someone _____ the back window. Do you hear it, too?
      A. trying open   B. trying to open   C. try opening   D. try to open

_____ 3. When Alan was questioned by the police, he admitted knowing about the embezzlement of funds from his company, but denied _____ in any way.
      A. to be involved   B. involving
      C. having involved   D. being involved

_____ 4. Mr. Lee was upset by _____ him the truth.
      A. our not having told   B. us not tell
      C. we didn't tell   D. not to tell

_____ 5. We considered _____ after work.
      A. to go shop   B. going shopping
      C. going to shop   D. to go to shop

_____ 6. Jack offered _____ care of my garden while I was out of town.
      A. take   B. taking   C. to have taken   D. to take

_____ 7. Could you please come over? I need you _____ the refrigerator.
      A. help me moving   B. helping me to move
      C. to help me move   D. help me to move

_____ 8. I just heard that there's been a major accident that has all of the traffic tied up. If we want to get to the play on time, we'd better avoid _____ the highway.
      A. having taken   B. take   C. to take   D. taking

_____ 9. The painting was beautiful. I stood there _____ it for a long time.
      A. for admiring   B. being admired   C. admire   D. admiring

_____ 10. Jim should have asked for help instead _____ to do it himself.
      A. of trying   B. to try   C. try   D. from trying

_____ 11. A plane with an engine on fire approached the runway. _____ was frightening. There could have been a terrible accident.
      A. Watch it landing   B. Watching it land
      C. To watch it to land   D. Watching to land it

_____ 12. The customs officer opened the suitcase _____ if anything illegal was being brought into the country.
      A. seeing   B. for seeing   C. see   D. to see

_____ 13. Sometimes very young children have trouble _____ fact from fiction and may believe that dragons actually exist.
      A. to separate   B. separating
      C. to be separated   D. for separating

_____ 14. Do you have an excuse _____ late to class two days in a row?
      A. for to be   B. for being   C. to be   D. being

_____ 15. Jack made me _____ him next week.
      A. to promise to call   B. to promise calling
      C. promise to call   D. promise calling

_____ 16. I got Barbara _____ her car for the weekend.
          A. to let me to borrow   B. let me borrow
          C. to let me borrow   D. let me to borrow

_____ 17. I'll never forget _____ that race. What a thrill!
          A. to win   B. win   C. being won   D. winning

_____ 18. No one has better qualifications. Carol is certain _____ for the job.
          A. to choose   B. having chosen   C. to be chosen   D. being chosen

_____ 19. I was enjoying my book, but I stopped _____ a program on TV
          A. reading to watch   B. to read to watch
          C. to read for watching   D. reading for to watch

_____ 20. Who is the woman talking to Mr. Quinn? I don't recall _____ her around the office before.
          A. to have seen   B. seeing   C. to see   D. being seen

◇ PRACTICE TEST B—GUIDED STUDY: Gerunds and infinitives. (Chapter 4)

Directions: Choose the correct answer.

Example:

__C__   _The office staff decided _____ a retirement party for Dolores._
          A. having had   B. to have had   C. to have   D. having

_____ 1. Roger proved that the accident wasn't his fault by _____ two witnesses who testified in his favor.
          A. produce   B. produced   C. to produce   D. producing

_____ 2. The front door is warped from the humidity. We have a difficult time _____ it.
          A. open   B. to open   C. having opened   D. opening

_____ 3. I stood up at the meeting and demanded _____. At last, I got the chance to express my opinion.
          A. to be heard   B. to hear   C. to have heard   D. to have heard

_____ 4. Did you ever finish _____ the office for that new client of yours?
          A. to design   B. designing
          C. designed   D. having designed

_____ 5. It's a beautiful day, and I have my brother's boat. Would you like to go _____?
          A. to sail   B. sailing   C. to sailing   D. for sailing

_____ 6. I called a plumber _____ the kitchen sink.
          A. for repairing   B. for to repair   C. to repair   D. to be repaired

_____ 7. I'm angry because you didn't tell me the truth. I don't like _____.
          A. deceiving   B. to deceive
          C. being deceived   D. having deceived

_____ 8. A good teacher makes her students _____ the world from new perspectives.
          A. to view   B. viewing   C. view   D. to be viewed

_____ 9. Please remember _____ your hand during the test if you have a question.
          A. raising   B. to raise   C. having raised   D. to have raised

_____ 10. It is important _____ care of your health.
          A. to take   B. to be taken   C. take   D. taken

_____ 11. _____ in restaurants as often as they do is very expensive.
          A. Being eaten   B. Having eaten
          C. Having been eating   D. Eating

_____ 12. I expect Mary _____ here early tonight. She should arrive in the next half hour.
     A. to come   B. coming   C. having come   D. to have come

_____ 13. I advised my niece not _____ at an early age.
     A. marrying   B. to marry
     C. being married   D. to have been married

_____ 14. Shhh. I hear someone _____ in the distance. Do you hear it, too?
     A. shout   B. shouted   C. to shout   D. shouting

_____ 15. I don't understand _____ your job so suddenly. Why did you do that?
     A. your quitting   B. you to have quit
     C. to quit   D. you quit

_____ 16. Last night, we saw a meteor _____ through the sky.
     A. streaked   B. to streak
     C. streak   D. to have streaked

_____ 17. My parents wouldn't let me _____ up late when I was a child.
     A. to be stay   B. staying   C. to stay   D. stay

_____ 18. Children should be encouraged _____ their individual interests.
     A. develop   B. to be developed
     C. to develop   D. developing

_____ 19. This room is too dark. We need _____ a lighter shade.
     A. to have it painted   B. to be painted
     C. painting it   D. to have it paint

_____ 20. I'm sorry I never graduated. I've always regretted not _____ college.
     A. to finish   B. finish
     C. finished   D. having finished

APPENDIX *1*
Supplementary Grammar Units

◇ **PRACTICE 1—SELFSTUDY:** Subjects, verbs, and objects. (Chart A-1)

Directions: Find the subject (**S**), verb (**V**), and object of the verb (**O**) in each sentence.

         S   **V**   **O**
1. The <u>politician</u> <u>supported</u> new <u>taxes.</u>

2. The mechanic repaired the engine.

3. Those boxes contain old photographs.

4. The teacher canceled the test.

5. An earthquake destroyed the village.

6. All birds have feathers.

List all of the nouns in the above sentences:

_politician, taxes,______

◇ **PRACTICE 2—SELFSTUDY:** Transitive vs. intransitive verbs. (Chart A-1)

Directions: Find the verb in each sentence. Write **VT** if it is transitive. Write **VI** if it is intransitive.

           VT
1. Mr. West <u>repeated</u> his question.

          VI
2. Smoke <u>rises.</u>

3. The children divided the candy.

4. I sneezed.

5. A strange thing happened.

6. The customer bought some butter.

7. Our team won the game.

8. Our team won yesterday.

9. Alice arrived at six o'clock.

10. I waited for Sam at the airport for two hours.

11. They're staying at a resort hotel in San Antonio, Texas.

12. The wind is blowing hard today.

13. I agree with you.

14. I walked to the theater, but Janice rode her bicycle.

◇ PRACTICE 3—SELFSTUDY: Identifying prepositions. (Chart A-2)

Directions: Find the prepositional phrases in the following. Identify the preposition (**P**) and the noun that is used as the object of the preposition (**O of P**).

                                                   P   **O of P**

1. Grasshoppers destroyed the wheat   <u>in</u> the <u>field.</u>

2. The waiter cleared the dirty dishes from our table.

3. I parked my car in the garage.

4. Trees fell during the violent storm.

5. Cowboys depended on horses for transportation.

6. We walked to the park after class.

◇ PRACTICE 4—SELFSTUDY: Sentence elements. (Charts A-1 and A-2)

Directions: Find the subjects (**S**), verbs (**VT** or **VI**), objects of verbs (**O**), and prepositional phrases (**PP**) in the following sentences.

           S   **VT**   **O**   **PP**
1. <u>Alex</u> <u>needs</u> new <u>batteries</u> <u>for his camera.</u>
           S   **VI**   **PP**
2. A <u>bomb</u> <u>exploded</u> <u>in the road.</u>

3. Sally wore her blue suit to the meeting.

4. Jim came to class without his books.

5. Dark clouds appeared on the horizon.

6. Plants need a reliable supply of water.

7. Mary filled the shelves of the cabinet with boxes of old books.

8. We enjoyed the view of snowy mountains from the window of our hotel room.

9. The child sat between her parents on the sandy beach. Above her, an eagle flew across the cloudless sky.

◇ PRACTICE 5—SELFSTUDY: Nouns, verbs, adjectives, adverbs. (Charts A-1 → A-4)

Directions: Identify the adjectives (**ADJ**) and adverbs (**ADV**) in the following sentences.

          ADJ   **ADV**   **ADJ**
1. A <u>terrible</u> fire spread <u>rapidly</u> through the <u>old</u> house.

2. A small child cried noisily in the third row of the theater.

3. The eager player waited impatiently for the start of the game.

4. An unusually large crowd came to the concert.

5. Arthur carefully repaired the antique vase with special glue.

6. On especially busy days, the telephone in the main office rings constantly.

The above six sentences have 10 adjectives and 7 adverbs.
Count the total number of nouns in the above six sentences: _____
Count the total number of verbs in the above six sentences: _____

◇ **PRACTICE 6—SELFSTUDY:** Adjectives and adverbs. (Charts A-3 and A-4)

Directions: Complete the sentence with the correct word (*adjective* or *adverb*).

1. *quick, quickly*   We ate __*quickly*__ and ran to the theater.

2. *quick, quickly*   We had a __*quick*__ dinner and ran to the theater.

3. *polite, politely*   I've always found Fred to be a _____ person.

4. *polite, politely*   He responded to my question _____.

5. *regular, regularly*   Mr. Thomas comes to the store _____ for cheese and bread.

6. *regular, regularly*   He is a _____ customer.

7. *usual, usually*   The teacher arrived at the _____ time.

8. *usual, usually*   She _____ comes to class five minutes before it begins.

9. *good, well*   Jennifer Cooper paints _____.

10. *good, well*   She is a _____ artist.

11. *gentle, gently*   A _____ breeze touched my face.

12. *gentle, gently*   A breeze _____ touched my face.

13. *annual, annually*   Many birds migrate _____ to a warm climate for the winter.

14. *annual, annually*   Many birds fly long distances in their _____ migration to a warm climate for the winter.

15. *bad, badly*   The audience booed the actors' _____ performance.

16. *bad, badly*   The audience booed and whistled because the actors performed _____ throughout the show.

◇ **PRACTICE 7—SELFSTUDY:** Midsentence adverbs. (Chart A-4)

Directions: Put the adverb in parentheses in its usual midsentence position.

                                  always

1. *(always)*   Sue ∧ takes a walk in the morning.

2. *(always)*   Tim is a hard worker.

3. *(always)*   Beth has worked hard.

4. *(always)*   Jack works hard.

5. *(always)*   Do you work hard?

6. *(usually)*   Taxis are available at the airport.

7. *(rarely)*   Tom takes a taxi to his office.

8. *(often)*   I have thought about quitting my job and sailing to Alaska.

9. *(probably)*   Cindy needs some help.

10. *(ever)*   Have you attended the show at the planetarium?

11. *(seldom)*   Al goes out to eat at a restaurant.

12. *(hardly ever)*   The students are late.

13. *(usually)*   Do you finish your homework before dinner?

14. *(generally)*   In India, the monsoon season begins in April.

15. *(usually)*   During the monsoon season, Mr. Singh's hometown receives around 610 centimeters (240 inches) of rain, an unusually large amount.

◇ **PRACTICE 8—SELFSTUDY: Linking verbs. (Charts A-1 → A-6)**

Directions: Some of the italicized words in the following are used as linking verbs. Identify which ones are linking verbs by underlining them. Also underline the adjective that follows the linking verb.

1. Olga *looked* at the fruit. *(no underline)*

2. It *looked* fresh.

3. Dan *noticed* a scratch on the door of his car.

4. Morris *tasted* the candy.

5. It *tasted* good.

6. The crowd *grew* quiet as the official began her speech.

7. Felix *grows* tomatoes in his garden.

8. Sally *grew* up in Florida.

9. I can *smell* the chicken in the oven.

10. It *smells* delicious.

11. Barbara *got* a package in the mail.

12. Al *got* sleepy after dinner.

13. During the storm, the sea *became* rough.

14. Nicole *became* a doctor after many years of study.

15. Diana *sounded* her horn to warn the driver of the other car.

16. Helen *sounded* happy when I talked to her.

17. The weather *turns* hot in July.

18. When Bob entered the room, I *turned* around to look at him.

19. I *turned* a page in the book.

20. It *appears* certain that Mary Hanson will win the election.

21. Dick's story *seems* strange. Do you believe it?

◇ **PRACTICE 9—SELFSTUDY: Linking verbs; adjectives and adverbs. (Charts A-3 → A-6)**

Directions: Complete the sentence with the correct word (*adjective* or *adverb*).

1. *clean, cleanly*   The floor looks ___*clean*___.

2. *slow, slowly*   The bear climbed ___*slowly*___ up the tree.

3. *safe, safely*   The plane landed _____ on the runway.

4. *anxious, anxiously*   When the wind started to blow, I grew _____.

5. *complete, completely* This list of names appears _____. No more names need to be added.

6. *wild, wildly* The crowd yelled _____ when we scored a goal.

7. *honest, honestly* The merchant looked _____, but she wasn't. I discovered when I got home that she had cheated me.

8. *thoughtful, thoughtfully* Jane looked at her book _____ before she answered the teacher's question.

9. *good, well* Most of the students did _____ on their tests.

10. *fair, fairly* The contract offer sounded _____ to me, so I accepted the job.

11. *terrible, terribly* Jim felt _____ about forgetting his son's birthday.

12. *good, well* A rose smells _____.

13. *light, lightly* As dawn approached, the sky became _____.

14. *confident, confidently* Beth spoke _____ when she delivered her speech.

15. *famous, famously* The actor became _____ throughout much of the world.

16. *fine, finely* I don't think this milk is spoiled. It tastes _____ to me.

◇ PRACTICE 10—GUIDED STUDY: Nouns, verbs, adjectives, adverbs, prepositions.
(Charts A-1 → A-6)

Directions: Identify each underlined word as a NOUN, VERB, ADJECTIVE, ADVERB, or PREPOSITION.

    PREP.   **NOUN**

1. <u>Through</u> the centuries, many people have confused <u>whales</u> with fish.

2. <u>Whales</u> are <u>mammals</u>, not fish. They <u>breathe</u> <u>air</u> and give live birth to their young.

3. Orca whales, which are black and white, are <u>highly</u> <u>trainable</u>. They are also called "killer whales," but trainers tell us that these whales are <u>intelligent</u> and <u>sensitive</u>. One time, a newly captured male orca <u>refused</u> to eat for a long time. <u>Finally</u>, he took a fish from the trainer. However, he didn't eat the fish <u>immediately</u>; he <u>took</u> it to another recently captured whale, a female who had also refused to eat, and <u>shared</u> it with her.

4. Some species of whales <u>dive</u> <u>deeply</u> <u>beneath</u> the <u>surface</u> of the ocean in order to feed and can stay <u>under</u> the <u>water</u> for more than an hour. All whales, however, must come to the surface <u>for</u> air.

5. Whales make the longest <u>migrations</u> known <u>among</u> mammals. Gray whales <u>swim</u> <u>from</u> the Pacific coast of Mexico, where they give birth in winter, <u>to</u> the <u>icy</u> Arctic for the summer.

6. Whales do not have vocal chords, but they can communicate <u>with</u> each other. They have a <u>wide</u> range of <u>clicks</u>, <u>whistles</u>, and <u>songs</u>. When a whale is captured in a net, other whales <u>gather</u> <u>around</u> it and <u>communicate</u> <u>through</u> the net. They follow the captured whale for long distances.

◇ PRACTICE 11—SELFSTUDY: Personal pronouns. (Chart A-7)

Directions: Choose the correct pronoun in italics.

1. Please take these papers and give   *it, them*   to Mike.

2. Tom asked Ann and   *I, me*   about the new theater.

3. Janice and   *I, me*   live in an apartment.

4. Just between you and   *I, me* , I think Tom is going to lose   *him, his*   job.

5. When a player committed a foul, the referee blew   *him, his*   whistle and pointed at   *she, her.*

6. A boa constrictor, which is a very large snake, kills   *its, it's*   victims by strangling   *it, them.*

7. People can easily send a letter to another city.   *It, They*   simply have to drop   *it, them*   into a collection box.

8. The teacher said to the students, "Throughout the semester, please write   *your, yours*   compositions on every other line, and be sure to write   *it, them*   in ink."

9. Both Ron and   *I, me*   are expecting some mail. Are those letters for   *he, him*   or   *I, me* ?

10. *My, Mine*   roommate and   *I, me*   have to share a bookshelf.   *She, Her*   keeps   *her, hers*   books on the top two shelves, and I keep   *my, mine*   on the bottom two shelves.

11. *Our, Ours*   house is almost the same as   *our, ours*   neighbors' house. The only difference in appearance is that   *our, ours*   is gray and   *their, theirs*   is white.

12. When I was in Florida, I observed an interesting fish-eating bird called an anhinga.   *It, they*   dives into the water and spears   *it's, its*   prey on   *it's, its*   long, pointed bill. Upon emerging from the water,   *it, they*   will toss a fish into the air and catch   *it, them*   in mid-air, swallowing   *it, them*   headfirst.   *It's, Its*   interesting to watch anhingas in action. I enjoy watching   *it, them.*

◇ PRACTICE 12—SELFSTUDY: Personal pronouns, error analysis. (Chart A-7)

Directions: Find and correct the errors in pronoun usage in the following.

1. Some North American food is very good, but I don't like most of them.

2. When we were schoolgirls, my sister and me used to play badminton after school every day.

3. If you want to pass your exams, you had better study very hard for it.

4. The work had to be finished by my boss and I after the store had closed for the night.

5. A hippopotamus spends most of it's time in the water of rivers and lakes.

6. I studied English when I was in high school. But I haven't studied it since I graduated from high school ten years ago, so I've forgotten a lot of them.

7. I looked everywhere in my room for my keys, but I couldn't find it.

8. After work, Mr. Gray asked to speak to Tim and I about the company's new policies. He explained it to us and asked for ours opinions.

9. The first person I saw when I got off the plane was my sister. My father and her had come to the airport to greet me. My father was waiting for we in his car outside the airport.

10. A child should learn to respect other people. They need to learn how to treat other people nicely, including their playmates.

11. My friends asked to borrow my car because their's was in the garage for repairs.

◇ **PRACTICE 13—SELFSTUDY:** Contractions. (Chart A-8)

Directions: Write the contraction of the pronoun and verb if appropriate. Write Ø if the pronoun and verb cannot be contracted.

1. He is (____*He's*____) in my class.

2. He was (____Ø____) in my class.

3. He has (__*He's*__) been here since July.

4. He has (____Ø____) a dog.*

5. She had (_____) been there for a long time before we arrived.

6. She had (_____) a bad cold.

7. She would (_____) like to go to the zoo.

8. I did (_____) well on the test.

9. We will (_____) be there early.

10. They (_____) in their seats over there.**

11. It is (_____) going to be hot tomorrow.

12. It has (_____) been a long time since I've seen him.

13. A bear is a large animal. It has (_____) four legs and brown hair.

14. We were (_____) on time.

15. We are (_____) always on time.

16. She has (_____) a good job.

17. She has (_____) been working there for a long time.

18. She had (_____) opened the window before class began.

19. She would (_____) have helped us if we had (_____) asked her.

20. He could (_____) have helped us if he had (_____) been there.

_____
*NOTE: **has, have,** and **had** are NOT contracted when they are used as main verbs. They are contracted only when they are used as helping verbs.
They're, their, and **there** all have the same pronunciation.

Directions: From the underlined sentences, make questions for the given answers. Fill in the blank space with the appropriate words. If no word is needed, write Ø.

1. Bob can live there.

	Question word	Auxiliary verb	Subject	Main verb	Rest of question	→	Answer
1a.	Ø	**Can**	Bob	**live**	there ?	→	Yes.
1b.	Where	**can**	Bob	**live**	Ø ?	→	There.
1c.	Who	**can**	Ø	**live**	there ? ?	→	Bob.

2. Don is living there.

	Question word	Auxiliary verb	Subject	Main verb	Rest of question	→	Answer
2a.	Ø		Don		there ? ?	→	Yes.
2b.	Where		Don		Ø ?	→	There.
2c.	Who		Ø		there ? ?	→	Don.

3. Sue lives there.

	Question word	Auxiliary verb	Subject	Main verb	Rest of question	→	Answer
3a.	Ø		Sue		there ? ?	→	Yes.
3b.	Where				Ø ?	→	There.
3c.	Who				there ? ?	→	Sue.

4. Ann will live there.

	Question word	Auxiliary verb	Subject	Main verb	Rest of question	→	Answer
4a.	Ø				there ? ?	→	Yes.
4b.	Where				Ø ?	→	There.
4c.	Who				there ? ?	→	Ann.

5. Jack lived there.

	Question word	Auxiliary verb	Subject	Main verb	Rest of question	→	Answer
5a.	Ø				there ? ?	→	Yes.
5b.					Ø ?	→	There.
5c.					there ? ?	→	Jack.

6. Mary has lived there.

	Question word	Auxiliary verb	Subject	Main verb	Rest of question	→	Answer
6a.					?	→	Yes.
6b.					?	→	There.
6c.					?	→	Mary.

Directions: Make questions to fit the dialogues. There are two speakers in each dialogue: A and B. Notice in the examples that in each dialogue there is a short answer and then in parentheses a long answer. The question you create should produce those answers.

1. A: ___*When are you going to the zoo?*___

   B: Tomorrow. *(I'm going to the zoo tomorrow.)*

2. A: ___*Are you going downtown later today?*___

   B: Yes. *(I'm going downtown later today.)*

3. A: _____

   B: Yes. *(I live in an apartment.)*

4. A: _____

   B: In a condominium. *(Sue lives in a condominium.)*

5. A: _____

   B: Jack. *(Jack lives in that house.)*

6. A: _____

   B: Yes. *(I can speak French.)*

7. A: _____

   B: Don. *(Don can speak Arabic.)*

8. A: _____

   B: Two weeks ago. *(Olga arrived two weeks ago.)*

9. A: _____

   B: Ali. *(Ali arrived late.)*

10. A: _____

    B: The window. *(Ann is opening the window.)*

11. A: _____

    B: Opening the window. *(Ann is opening the window.)*

12. A: _____

    B: Her book. *(Mary opened her book.)*

13. A: _____

    B: Tom. *(Tom opened the door.)*

14. A: _____

    B: Yes. *(The mail has arrived.)*

15. A: _____

    B: Yes. *(I have a bicycle.)*

16. A: _____

    B: A pen. *(Alex has a pen in his hand.)*

17. A: _____

    B: Yes. *(I like ice cream.)*

18. A: _____

    B: Yes. *(I would like an ice cream cone.)*

19. A: _____

    B: A candy bar. *(Joe would like a candy bar.)*

20. A: _____

    B: Ann. *(Ann would like a soft drink.)*

◇ **PRACTICE 16—SELFSTUDY:** Yes/no and information questions. (Charts B-1 and B-2).

Directions: Make questions to fit the dialogues. There are two speakers in each dialogue: A and B. Notice in the examples that in each dialogue there is a short answer and then in parentheses a long answer. The question you create should produce those answers.

1. A: **_How long has Pierre been living here?_**

    B: Since last September. *(Pierre has been living here since last September.)*

2. A: I need some information. Maybe you can help me. **_Which (city) is_**
       farther north, London or Paris?

    B: London. *(London is farther north than Paris.)*

3. A: Is that your umbrella?

    B: No.

    A: _____

    B: Jane's. *(It's Jane's.)*

4. A: I haven't seen you for weeks. How are you? _____

    B: Going to school and studying hard. *(I've been going to school and studying hard.)*

5. A: Did you call Sally?

    B: Yes, but she wasn't in.

    A: _____

    B: Her roommate. *(Her roommate answered the phone.)*

6. A: Do the villagers have tractors in the rural areas?

    B: No. They don't have any modern farm machinery.

    A: _____

    B: With oxen or water buffaloes. *(They plow their fields with oxen or water buffaloes.)*

7. A: I really like having my own computer.

    B: _____

    A: Since last December. *(I've had it since last December.)*

8. A: _____ I've never seen one quite like it.

    B: A myna. It's common in warm climates. *(That kind of bird is a myna.)*

9. A: _____

    B: I missed my bus. *(I was late for work this morning because I missed my bus.)*

10. A: Last summer we painted the outside of our house.
    B: That must have been a big job. _____
    A: About four days. (It took us about four days.)

11. A: Jack was late last night, wasn't he? _____
    B: At 11:30. (He finally got home at 11:30.)

12. A: Would you like a cup of coffee?
    B: Thanks. That sounds good.
    A: _____
    B: With cream and sugar. (I take it with cream and sugar.)

13. A: _____
    B: Around 250 million. (The population of the United States is around 250 million.)

14. A: _____
    B: The red one. (Of those two coats, I like the red one better than the black one.)

15. A: We spent a relaxing weekend in a small village in the mountains.
    B: _____
    A: By bus. (We got there by bus.)

16. A: I'm sending a letter to the consulate about the problem I'm having with my visa. _____
    _____
    B: Mr. Ho. (You should address it to Mr. Ho.)

17. A: _____
    B: Over 800 miles. (It's over 800 miles from here to Los Angeles.)

18. A: _____
    B: Ann, Susan, and Alice. (Ann, Susan, and Alice are going to be at the meeting tonight.)

19. A: In my country, we eat rice every day. _____
    B: About once a week. (People in my country have rice about once a week.)

20. A: _____
    B: Silly looking hat?! I think it's a great hat! I got it at the shopping mall. (I got that silly looking
    hat at the shopping mall.)

21. A: _____
    B: Twelve. (There are twelve edges on a cube.)
    A: _____
    B: Eight. (There are eight edges on a pyramid.)

22. A: _____
    B: To say you're sorry. ("Apologize" means "to say you're sorry.")

23. A: I've never met Bob. _____
    B: He has dark hair, a mustache, wears glasses, and is about average height.

24. A: You know Ann Green, don't you? _____
    B: She's energetic, bright, very friendly. A really nice person.

Directions: Make questions from the following sentences. The italicized words in parentheses should be the answer to your question.

1. I take my coffee *(black)*. → *How do you take your coffee?*

2. I have *(an English-English)* dictionary.

3. He *(runs a grocery store)* for a living.

4. Margaret was talking to *(her uncle)*.

5. *(Only ten)* people showed up for the meeting.

6. *(Due to heavy fog)*, none of the planes could take off.

7. She was thinking about *(her experiences as a rural doctor)*.

8. I was driving *(sixty-five miles per hour)* when the policeman stopped me.

9. I like *(hot and spicy Mexican)* food best.

10. *(The)* apartment *(at the end of the hall on the second floor)* is mine.

11. Oscar is *(friendly, generous, and kindhearted)*.

12. Oscar *(is tall and thin and has short black hair)*.

13. *(Ann's)* dictionary fell to the floor.

14. Abby isn't here *(because she has a doctor's appointment)*.

15. All of the students in the class will be informed of their final grades *(on Friday)*.

16. I feel *(awful)*.

17. Of those three books, I preferred *(the one by Tolstoy)*.

18. I like *(rock)* music.

19. The plane is expected to be *(an hour)* late.

20. The driver of the stalled car lit a flare *(in order to warn oncoming cars)*.

21. I want *(the felt-tip)* pen, *(not the ballpoint)*.

22. The weather is *(hot and humid)* in July.

23. I like my steak *(medium rare)*.

24. I did *(very well)* on the test.

25. There are *(31,536,000)* seconds in a year.

◇ PRACTICE 18—GUIDED STUDY: Information questions. (Charts B-1 and B-2)

Directions: Make questions from the given sentences. (Suggestion: Ask a classmate or friend to read what is written for each item. Then you, with your book closed, make an appropriate question.)

1. The teacher. The teacher opened the door. → *Who opened the door?*

2. Talking on the phone. Bob is talking on the phone. → *What is Bob doing?*

3. My friend. That letter is from my friend.

4. Mary. Mary wrote that letter.

5. My mother's. That is my mother's coat.

6. In August. Alice and John are going to get married in August.

7. Ours. Our team won, not their team.

8. Gray. Her eyes are gray.

9. Black. Her hair is black.

10. Herb tea. That kind of tea is herb tea.

11. Coffee. I usually drink coffee with my breakfast.

12. Ten minutes. It usually takes me ten minutes to eat breakfast.

13. By taxi. I got to the airport by taxi.

14. Four. I have four brothers and sisters.

15. Florida. I grew up in Florida.

16. Five hours. It takes five hours to get there by plane.

17. Historical novels. I like to read historical novels.

18. Chapters 2 and 3. The test will cover Chapters 2 and 3.

19. Because he wanted to travel around the world. Frank quit school because he wanted to travel around the world.

20. For three days. She's been sick for three days.

21. Twenty. I'm going to invite twenty people to my party.

22. This one. You should buy this camera, not that one.

23. Marie Curie. Marie Curie discovered radium.

24. Practicing asking questions. I'm practicing asking questions.

25. Great. Everything's going great.

◇ **PRACTICE 19—GUIDED STUDY: Information questions. (Charts B-1 and B-2)**

Directions: Create dialogues between A and B in which the following are the answers to questions. Make up any question that would produce the given answer.

Example:
  Next week.
    A: *When are we going to have a test on this chapter?*
    B: *Next week.*

1. Blue.
2. Two years.
3. Cold and wet.
4. The one on the red chair.
5. Chris's.
6. With two "t's".
7. Andy and Ed.
8. Two million.
9. Once a week.
10. Five blocks.

11. 1979.
12. Fine.
13. Biochemistry.
14. Reading.
15. Saudi Arabia.
    In the Middle East.
    Over eight million.
    Islam.
    Oil.
    Riyadh.

Directions: Pair up with another student. Together create a dialogue for the given situation in one or more of the following. One of you is Speaker A and the other is Speaker B. (Note to the student: If you don't have a partner, write dialogues as you would imagine the conversation to go.) The beginning of each dialogue is given.

1. *The following conversation takes place after class is over.*
   Speaker A, you are a student. You have a problem.
   Speaker B, you are a teacher. You try to solve the problem.

   A: Excuse me, _____. Do you have a few minutes?

   B: Certainly.

   A: I'd like to talk to you about _____.

   B: _____.

       etc.

2. *The following conversation takes place on the telephone.*
   Speaker A, you work for a travel agency.
   Speaker B, you want to take a trip.

   A: Hello. Worldwide Travel Agency. May I help you?

   B: Yes. I need to make arrangements to go to _____.

       (etc.)

3. *The following conversation takes place at a department store.*
   Speaker A, you are a salesperson.
   Speaker B, you are trying to decide whether or not to buy something.

   A: Could I help you?

   B: Yes. I'm thinking about buying _____, but _____.

       (etc.)

4. *The following conversation takes place at a job interview.*
   Speaker A, you are the interviewer.
   Speaker B, you are the interviewee.

   A: Mr./Ms. _____, isn't it?

   B: Yes.

   A: I'm Mr./Ms. _____. It's nice to meet you. Come in and have a seat.

       (etc.)

5. *Assign yourselves roles, and make up your own conversation.*

◇ PRACTICE 21—GUIDED STUDY: Shortened yes/no questions. (Chart B-1)

Directions: Sometimes in spoken English, the auxiliary and the subject **you** are dropped from a yes/no question. Notice the following examples:
   (a) Going to bed now? = Are you going to bed now?
   (b) Finish your work? = Did you finish your work?
   (c) Want to go to the movie with us? = Do you want to go to the movie with us?
Find the shortened questions in the following, and then give the complete question form.

1. A: Need some help?
   B: Thanks.

2. A: Why do you keep looking out of the window? Expecting someone?
   B: I'm waiting for the mail.
3. A: You look tired.
   B: I am.
   A: Stay up late last night?
   B: Yup.
4. A: I'm looking forward to going to Colorado over spring vacation.
   B: Ever been there before?
5. A: Why are you pacing the floor? Nervous?
   B: Who me?
6. A: Want a cup of coffee?
   B: Only if it's already made.
7. A: Heard any news about your scholarship?
   B: Not yet.
8. A: Hungry?
   B: Yeah. You?

◇ PRACTICE 22—SELFSTUDY: Negative questions. (Chart B-3)

Directions: In the following dialogues, make negative questions from the words in parentheses, and determine the expected response.

1. A: Your infected finger looks terrible. *(You, see, not)* __***Haven't you seen***__ a doctor yet?

   B: __***No***__. But I'm going to. I don't want the infection to get any worse.

2. A: I can't understand why David isn't here yet. *(He, say, not)* _____ he

   would be here by 4:00?

   B: _____. Something must have delayed him. I'm sure he'll be here soon.

3. A: Did you see Mark at the meeting?

   B: No, I didn't.

   A: Really? *(He, be, not)* _____ there?

   B: _____.

   A: That's funny. I've never known him to miss a meeting before.

4. A: Why didn't you come to the meeting yesterday afternoon?

   B: What meeting? I didn't know there was a meeting.

   A: *(Mary, tell, not)* _____ you about it?

   B: _____. No one said a word to me about it.

5. A: What's the matter? Everyone else at the party seems to be having fun, but you look bored.

   (You, have, not) _____ a good time?

   B: _____. I'm thinking about going home pretty soon.

6. A: I have a package for Janet. *(Janet and you, work, not)* _____

   _____ in the same building?

   B: _____. I'd be happy to take the package to her tomorrow when I go to work.

7. A: Frank didn't report all of his income on his tax forms.

   B: *(That, be, not)* _____ against the law?

   A: _____. And that's why he's in a lot of legal trouble. He might even go to jail.

8. A: Did you know that the Missouri River is the longest river in the United States?

   B: Are you sure? *(The Mississippi, be, not)* _____ the longest?

   A: _____. The Missouri is around 2,565 miles (4,130 kilometers) long. The Mississippi is around 2,350 miles (3,800 kilometers).

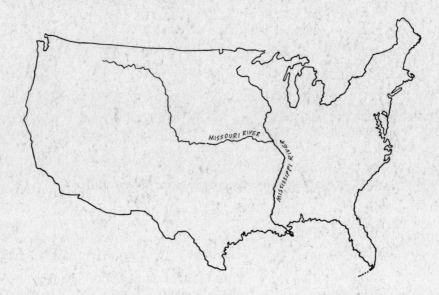

◇ **PRACTICE 23—SELFSTUDY: Tag questions. (Chart B-4)**

Directions: Add tag questions to the following.

1. You live in an apartment, __***don't you***__?

2. You've never been in Italy, __***have you***__?

3. Sally turned in her report, _____?

4. There are more countries north of the equator than south of it, _____?

5. You've never met Jack Freeman, _____?

6. You have a ticket to the game, _____?

7. You'll be there, _____?

8. Tom knows Alice Reed, _____?

9. We should call Rita, _____?

10. Monkeys can't sing, _____?

11. These books aren't yours, _____?

12. That's Bob's, _____?

13. No one died in the accident, _____?

14. I'm right, _____?

15. This grammar is easy, _____?

Directions: Complete the sentences with **not** or **no.**

1. There are ___*no*___ mountains in Iowa. You will ___*not*___ see any mountains in Iowa.

2. Fish have _____ eyelids. They are _____ able to shut their eyes, but they do rest or sleep regularly.

3. _____ automobiles are permitted in the park on Sundays.

4. I can do it by myself. I need _____ help.

5. The operation was _____ successful. The patient did _____ survive.

6. When I became ill, I had _____ choice but to cancel my trip.

7. The opera *Rigoletto* was _____ composed by Mozart; it was composed by Verdi.

8. I have _____ patience with cheaters.

9. Ask me _____ questions, and I'll tell you _____ lies.

10. You should _____ ask people embarrassing questions about their personal lives.

11. "Colour" is spelled with a "u" in British English, but there is _____ "u" in the American English spelling ("color").

12. I excitedly reeled in my fishing line, but the big fish I had expected to find did _____ appear. Instead, I pulled up an old rubber boot.

◇ **PRACTICE 25—SELFSTUDY: Avoiding "double negatives." (Chart C-2)**

Directions: Correct the errors in the following sentences, all of which contain double negatives.

1. We don't have no time to waste.

→ *We have no time to waste.*   OR: *We don't have any time to waste.*

2. I didn't have no problems.

3. I can't do nothing about it.

4. You can't hardly ever understand her when she speaks.

5. I don't know neither Ann nor her husband.

6. Don't never drink water from that river without boiling it first.

7. Because I had to sit in the back row of the auditorium, I couldn't barely hear the speaker.

◇ **PRACTICE 26—SELFSTUDY: Beginning a sentence with a negative word. (Chart C-3)**

Directions: Change each sentence so that it begins with a negative word.

1. I had hardly stepped out of bed when the phone rang.

→ *Hardly had I stepped out of bed when the phone rang.*

2. I will never say that again.

3. I have scarcely ever enjoyed myself more than I did yesterday.

4. She rarely makes a mistake.

5. I will never trust him again because he lied to me.

6. It is hardly ever possible to get an appointment to see him.

7. I seldom skip breakfast.

8. I have never known a more generous person than Samantha.

◇ **PRACTICE 27—SELFSTUDY: Using articles. (Charts D-1 and D-2)**

Directions: Complete the sentences with *a/an, the,* or Ø.

1. ___Ø___ lightning is ___*a*___ flash of light. It is usually followed by ___Ø___ thunder.

2. Last night we had ___*a*___ terrible storm. Our children were frightened by ___*the*___ thunder.

3. _____ circles are _____ round geometric figures.

4. _____ circle with _____ slash drawn through it is an international symbol meaning "Do not do this!" For example, _____ circle in _____ illustration below means "No smoking."

5. _____ milk I put on my cereal this morning was sour because someone forgot to put it in _____ refrigerator after dinner last night.

6. _____ milk is an important source of _____ protein and _____ calcium.

7. Do you ever gaze into _____ space and wonder if _____ other life forms exist in _____ universe?

8. We need to get _____ new phone.

9. Alex, would you please answer _____ phone?

10. _____ wisdom comes more from _____ understanding than from _____ knowledge.

11. I always appreciate _____ wisdom of my mother's advice.

12. In class yesterday, I sat next to two women. _____ woman on my right had _____ right answer to _____ teacher's question about verb forms.

13. Maria is _____ independent young woman who knows her own mind.

14. We flew to Dallas and then rented _____ car. On _____ second day we had _____ car, it wouldn't start, so the rental agency provided us with another one.

15. _____ people use _____ plants in _____ many different ways. Plants supply us with _____ oxygen. They are a source of _____ lifesaving medicines. We use plant products to build _____ houses and to make _____ paper and _____ textiles.

◇ **PRACTICE 28—GUIDED STUDY: Using articles. (Charts D-1 and D-2)**

Directions: Complete the sentences with *a/an, the,* or Ø.

1. Have you met Mr. and Mrs. Smith? Mrs. Smith used to be _____ teacher, but now she is _____ computer programmer. Mr. Smith is _____ architect. The Smiths used to live in _____ apartment, but recently they have built _____ house.

2. Frank Lloyd Wright is _____ name of _____ famous architect. He is _____ architect who designed the Guggenheim Museum in New York. He also designed _____ hotel in Tokyo. _____ hotel was designed to withstand _____ earthquakes.

3. When you look at _____ sandy shore, it might seem practically empty of _____ animals. This appearance is deceptive, however. Beneath _____ surface, the sand is full of _____ life. It is teeming with _____ crabs, _____ shrimp, _____ worms, _____ snails, and _____ other kinds of _____ marine animals.

4. Our children enjoyed going to the beach yesterday. When they dug in _____ sand, they found various kinds of _____ animals. Susie found _____ crab, and so did Johnny. _____ crab Johnny found pinched him, which made him cry. But he had _____ good time at _____ beach anyway.

5. The biggest bird in the world is the ostrich. It eats just about anything it can reach, including _____ stones, _____ glass, and _____ keys. It can kill _____ person with one kick.

6. In _____ recent newspaper article, I read about _____ Australian swimmer who was saved from _____ shark by _____ group of dolphins. When _____ shark attacked _____ swimmer, _____ dolphins chased it away. They saved _____ swimmer's life.

7. I heard on the radio that there is _____ evidence that _____ dolphins suffer in captivity. Dolphins that are free in _____ nature live around 40 years. Captive dolphins live _____ average of 12 years. It is believed that some captive dolphins commit _____ suicide.

8. According to today's paper, the mayor has appointed _____ committee to study what improvements need to be made in the city. _____ committee, which plans to continue its study through the rest of this year, will discuss _____ following proposals: (1) to build _____ new sewage disposal plant and (2) to create _____ new park. In _____ present proposal, _____ new park would have _____ swimming pool.

9. The large oak tree growing at _____ southeast corner of Vine Avenue and Pine Street has been _____ landmark since pioneer days. Unfortunately, it was shattered by _____ bolt of lightning during the thunderstorm last night.

10. My uncle's hobby is restoring _____ old cars. Right now he's working on _____ 1922 automobile. It's _____ antique car and has great value.

11. My aunt's new car has _____ power windows, _____ cassette player, and _____ multi-adjustable driver's seat.

12. Patty is my ten-year-old daughter. She likes to play _____ jokes on people. Yesterday she put _____ frog into _____ lunchbox she saw sitting on _____ table in _____ school lunchroom.

13. _____ most mirrors are made from _____ glass to which _____ thin layer of _____ silver or _____ aluminum has been applied.

14. Long-term exposure to _____ sun between _____ hours of 10 AM and 3 PM can be harmful. _____ person's skin will eventually become wrinkled and more susceptible to _____ cancer.

15. _____ phonograph records have become old-fashioned. They have been supplanted by _____ compact discs, which are commonly referred to as CDs.

16. Yesterday I locked my keys in my car. Using _____ coat hanger, I tried to reach _____ lock inside _____ window next to _____ driver's seat, but I couldn't get _____ door to unlock. I thought about calling _____ police, but finally decided to call my wife. I suggested she take _____ taxi and bring her keys to open _____ car for me.

17. Look. There's _____ fly walking on _____ ceiling. It's upside down. Do you suppose _____ fly was flying rightside up and flipped over at _____ last second, or was it flying upside down when it landed on _____ ceiling?

18. This sentence is _____ last sentence in this workbook. This is _____ end.

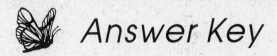 # Answer Key

WORKBOOK A
UNDERSTANDING AND USING ENGLISH GRAMMAR, SECOND EDITION

Answers to the Selfstudy Practices

To the student: To make it easy to correct your own answers, remove this answer key along the perforations, and make a separate answer key booklet for yourself.

Chapter 1: VERB TENSES

◇ **1 (p. 1):** 1. do you do . . . eat 2. did you do . . . ate . . . visited . . . wrote 3. are you doing . . . am talking . . . am answering 4. was looking 5. have I asked . . . have asked 6. have you been doing . . . have been talking 7. will you be (OR: are you going to be) . . . will be (OR: am going to be) 8. will you be doing . . . will be sitting 9. had you done . . . had eaten 10. will you have done . . . will have eaten

◇ **2 (p. 2):** 1. simple present 2. simple past 3. present progresive 4. past progressive 5. present perfect 6. present perfect progressive 7. simple future 8. future progressive 9. past perfect 10. future perfect 11. past perfect progressive 12. future perfect progressive

◇ **3 (p. 4):** 1. eats 2. ate 3. will eat (OR: is going to eat) 4. am eating 5. was eating 6. will be eating 7. have already eaten 8. had already eaten 9. will have already eaten (OR: will already have eaten) 10. has been eating 11. had been eating 12. will have been eating

◇ **4 (p. 6):**

PART A	PART B	PART C	PART D	PART E
1. shouting, shouted	11. pointing	21. bothered	31. dreaming	41. combed
2. sloping, sloped	12. beating	22. blurred	32. filing	42. wrapped
3. stopping, stopped	13. betting	23. scared	33. filling	43. groaned
4. stooping, stooped	14. exciting	24. scarred	34. failing	44. occupied
5. answering, answered	15. exiting	25. feared	35. annoying	45. sprayed
6. referring, referred	16. regretting	26. starred	36. denying	46. wiped
7. returning, returned	17. attempting	27. stared	37. scrubbing	47. whipped
8. enjoying, enjoyed	18. shouting	28. ordered	38. draining	48. accepted
9. copying, copied	19. flitting	29. suffered	39. fanning	49. permitted
10. dying, died	20. interesting	30. occurred	40. interrupting	50. merited
				51. whispered
				52. inferred

◇ **5 (p. 7):** 1. isn't shining   2. own   3. am trying   4. belongs   5. sleep   6. is bleeding   7. am failing   8. shrinks   9. is biting   10. isn't blowing   11. are always fighting   12. is he screaming   13. means   14. are you whispering   15. is taping

◇ **6 (p. 8):** 1. has   2. is having   3. weighs   4. is weighing...needs   5. am doing...consists   6. am thinking...think   7. is looking...look   8. is being...doesn't want...is always

◇ **9 (p. 13):** 1. swore   2. shook   3. drew   4. burst   5. hid   6. stuck   7. slit   8. slid   9. spread   10. won   11. dug   12. bought

◇ **10 (p. 13):** 1. bit   2. clung   3. meant   4. blew   5. quit   6. felt   7. stung   8. swam   9. paid   10. caught   11. shed   12. wove

◇ **11 (p. 14):** 1. spent   2. led   3. bet   4. wept   5. upset   6. split   7. sank   8. flew   9. spun   10. rang   11. chose   12. froze

◇ **12 (p. 15):** 1. fell   2. struck   3. broadcast   4. sought   5. lost   6. dealt   7. held   8. shot   9. cost   10. swept   11. stole   12. fled

◇ **14 (p. 16):** 1. raises   2. rose   3. set   4. sat   5. lays   6. lying   7. lay   8. laid   9. hung   10. lies   11. lies

◇ **15 (p. 16):** 1. had   2. were at home having   3. was in his garage working...exploded...caused...lit (OR: lighted)   4. didn't see...was thinking...were you thinking   5. didn't want...was waiting   6. didn't hear...was in her room listening   7. stopped...fell...spilled   8. came...didn't hear...was in her room drying   9. served...went   10. looked...was sleeping...was dreaming...was smiling

◇ **18 (p. 18):** 1. have already eaten   2. have won   3. haven't written   4. has improved   5. hasn't started   6. have already swept   7. have you known   8. have made   9. have never ridden   10. Have you ever swum   11. has grown   12. have driven   13. has forgotten   14. has cost...have saved

◇ **19 (p. 19):** 1. for...since   2. since   3. for   4. for...since   5. for   6. since   7. for   8. since   9. for...for   10. since   11. since...since   12. since

◇ **20 (p. 20):** 1. knew...have known   2. agreed...have agreed   3. took...has taken   4. has played ...played   5. wrote...has written   6. sent...have sent   7. has flown...flew   8. overslept...has overslept   9. has drawn...drew   10. has called...called   11. has worn...wore   12. has risen...rose

◇ **22 (p. 21):** 1. have been playing   2. has played   3. has been sleeping   4. has slept   5. haven't flown   6. have been flying   7. have been searching   8. has raised   9. has been lecturing   10. has never missed   11. have finally made...have chosen   12. has been driving

◇ **25 (p. 24):** 1. had already finished   2. turned on   3. had already invented   4. had burned   5. had never spent   6. stung   7. had never designed   8. helped   9. had never been   10. had flown   11. had not taught   12. had already left

◇ **26 (p. 24):** 1. went...had never been...didn't take...was   2. ate...had never eaten   3. was ...studied...had never had...spoke...enjoyed   4. saw...did...Had you ever acted ...started   5. went...moved...took...had arrived...laughed...invited...was   6. traveled...had never lived...had...became...had never lived   7. emigrated... had never traveled...settled...grew...went...had always wanted

◇ **28 (p. 26):**   1. had been listening to...have been dancing...singing   2. have been waiting   3. had been waiting   4. has been training   5. had been running   6. had been trying...has been teaching   7. has been performing   8. have been working...had been building

◇ **30 (p. 27):**   1. will   2. are going to   3. will   4. Are you going to...are going to   5. am going to   6. will   7. will   8. am going to

◇ **32 (p. 29):**   1. [when you arrive tomorrow.]   2.[After the rain stops,]   3. [before my wife gets home from work today.]   4.[As soon as the war is over,]   5. [until Jessica comes.]   6. [when the tide comes in,]

◇ **33 (p. 29):**   1. will not/are not going to return...get   2. gets...will be/is going to be   3. will lend ...finish   4. hear...will let   5. isn't going to be/won't be...learns...comes...asks   6. returns...will start/is going to start   7. is going to build/will build...will be/is going to be ...complete   8. will be/is going to be...is

◇ **35 (p. 30):**   1. am meeting   2. am taking   3. are having...are coming   4. am seeing   5. is picking up   6. are driving   7. is playing   8. am quitting

◇ **37 (p. 32):**   1. heals...will be playing   2. clear...will be standing   3. start...will be attending   4. have...will be shopping   5. will be attending...return   6. will be living...will be driving

◇ **38 (p. 33):**   1. will already have risen (OR: will have already risen)   2. will have been riding   3. will already have arrived (OR: will have already arrived)   4. will have been listening   5. will have smoked   6. will have been flying   7. will have saved   8. will have taught

◇ **40 (p. 34):**   1. had been   2. met   3. had missed   4. was   5. got   6. took   7. was   8. had grown   9. was   10. was wearing   11. had changed   12. was still   13. asked   14. had gained   15. had turned   16. looked   17. were

◇ **41 (p. 34):**   1. will have been   2. will meet   3. will have missed   4. will be   5. get   6. will take   7. will no longer be   8. will have grown   9. will be   10. will probably be wearing   11. will have changed   12. will still be   13. will ask   14. will probably have gained   15. will have turned   16. will look   17. will be

◇ **44 (p. 38):**   1. I **have been** studying....
2. ...to my country, I **will have been** away....
3. As soon as I **graduate**, I **am** going to return....
4. ...scientists will **have** discovered the cure....
5. ...but I **haven't met** the right....
6. I **have seen** that movie..., and now I **want** to see....
7. Last night, I **had** dinner with two friends. I **have known** both of....
8. I **do** not like my job....   I **think** he is right.
9. ...the teachers **have given** us....
10. There **have been** fewer than....   George Washington **was** the first....   He **became** the president....
11. ...when he **felt** a sharp....
12. ...I **used** my key....   I **tried** my key....   So I **knocked** on the door...the door **opened**, but I **didn't see** my wife....   I **had been trying**....   I quickly **apologized** and **went** to....

◇ **PRACTICE TEST A (p. 39):** 1. C   2. C   3. A   4. A   5. B   6. C   7. C   8. C   9. B
10. C   11. D   12. A   13. D   14. A   15. B   16. B   17. D
18. B   19. D   20. C

Chapter 2: MODAL AUXILIARIES AND SIMILAR EXPRESSIONS

◇ **1 (p. 43):** 1. C   2. C   3. C   4. B   5. C   6. C   7. C   8. C   9. C   10. C   11. C
12. C

◇ **2 (p. 44):** 1. Would you (please) hand me that book?   2. Could you (please) give me some advice about buying a computer?   3. Could I (please) borrow your wheelbarrow?   4. May I (please) have a cup of coffee?   5. Can I (please) use your bicycle tomorrow?   6. Would you (please) read over my composition for spelling errors?   7. Would you mind opening the door for me?
8. Would you mind if I left early?

◇ **3 (p. 44):** 1. opening   2. if I opened   3. taking   4. if I showed   5. drying   6. finishing
7. if I used   8. waiting   9. if I borrowed   10. if I gave

◇ **7 (p. 47):** 1. B   2. A   3. A   4. B   5. A   6. C   7. B   8. C   9. A   10. B

◇ **8 (p. 48):** 1. Do you have to . . . have to   2. had to . . . . Did you have to   3. doesn't have to
4. don't have to (OR: won't have to)   5. have had to   6. did Tom have to   7. don't have to (OR: won't have to)   8. Did John have to   9. has had to   10. will have had to
11. Don't you have to   12. will have to (OR: is going to have to) . . . . Does she have to (OR: Will she have to)   13. didn't have to   14. haven't had to

◇ **16 (p. 54):** 1. B   2. A   3. A   4. B   5. B   6. A   7. B   8. A   9. B   10. A   11. B
12. B

◇ **20 (p. 57):** 1. a. Fred   2. a. Jane   3. a. a rat   4. a. Mark   5. a. Janet   6. a. the breeze
b. Tom   b. Don   b. a cat   b. my neighbor   b. Sally   b. Bobby
c. Alice   c. Sue   c. a mouse   c. Carol   c. Bob   c. The cat
d. Ann   d. Andy

◇ **21 (p. 59):** 1. may have been attending   2. shouldn't be watching   3. might have been washing
4. must be waiting   5. shouldn't have left   6. could be visiting   7. should watch
8. must have thrown   9. should be working . . . shouldn't be wasting (OR: shouldn't waste)
10. might be traveling   11. might have borrowed   12. must be playing   13. might have been washing . . . may have already left   14. must not have been expecting (OR: must not have expected)

◇ **24 (p. 62):** 1. used to live   2. am used to living   3. used to work   4. am used to working   5. used to have . . . . am not used to seeing   6. used to think   7. used to take   8. is used to flying   9. used to give   10. is used to taking

◇ **26 (p. 63):** 1. would always yell . . . would come   2. would fall . . . would throw   3. would never call . . . wouldn't even knock   4. would always bring   5. would take   6. would always wipe
7. would tell . . . would listen   8. would drive

◇ **28 (p. 64):** 1. could stay   2. went (*could* is not possible)   3. managed to complete (*could* is not possible)   4. finished (*could* is not possible)   5. watched (*could* is not possible)   6. could ride   7. managed to get (*could* is not possible)   8. rode (*could* is not possible)   9. enjoyed (*could* is not possible)   10. got (*could* is not possible)   11. could swim

◇ **PRACTICE TEST A (p. 70):** 1. B   2. D   3. D   4. A   5. B   6. B   7. D   8. C   9. D
10. A   11. D   12. C   13. C   14. D   15. C   16. A   17. D
18. C   19. D   20. A

Chapter 3: THE PASSIVE

◇ **1 (p. 74):** 1. are 2. is being 3. has been 4. was 5. was being 6. had been 7. will be 8. is going to be 9. will have been 10. has been 11. was 12. are being 13. will be 14. had been 15. will have been 16. are 17. is going to be 18. were being

◇ **3 (p. 75):** 1. was...discovered 2. was written 3. won't be paid 4. was refilled 5. Was ...knocked 6. wasn't broken 7. am not impressed 8. is being taped 9. is...being flown 10. will be won 11. won't be influenced 12. is going to be decided 13. has been discovered 14. hasn't been taught 15. had...been delivered 16. was being affected

◇ **4 (p. 77):**

VERB	OBJECT OF VERB	PASSIVE SENTENCE
1. will pay	the bill	The bill will be paid by Al.
2. will come	Ø	Ø
3. supplies	towels	Towels are supplied by the hotel.
4. happen	Ø	Ø
5. noticed	my mistake	My mistake was noticed by everyone.
6. arrived	Ø	Ø
7. didn't surprise	me	I wasn't surprised by the news.
8. Did...surprise	you	Were you surprised by the news?
9. wasn't shining	Ø	Ø
10. interrupted	my story	My story was interrupted by Ann.
11. Do...exist	Ø	Ø
12. fly	Ø	Ø
13. Will...come	Ø	Ø
14. died	Ø	Ø
15. Did...throw	the ball	Was the ball thrown by Bob?
16. laughed	Ø	Ø
17. told	the story	The story was told by an old man.
18. rained	Ø	Ø

◇ **5 (p. 77):** 1. You will be met at the airport by my uncle. 2. (*no change*) 3. The food will be prepared by the chef. 4. (*no change*) 5. The fire wasn't caused by lightning. 6. (*no change*) 7. The subway is ridden by thousands of people every day. 8. (*no change*) 9. (*no change*) 10. (*no change*) 11. (*no change*) 12. The dispute is going to be settled by a special committee. 13. (*no change*) 14. (*no change*) 15. (*no change*) 16. Was the enemy surrounded by the army? 17. (*no change*) 18. Windmills were invented by the Persians around 1500 years ago. (OR: Windmills were invented around 1500 years ago by the Persians.)

◇ **6 (p. 78):** 1. will be notified 2. didn't remember 3. is being restored 4. was built 5. was ruled...walked...stood 6. is visited 7. do not use 8. do not agree 9. will be invaded (OR: are going to be invaded) 10. live...lives 11. Had you already been accepted 12. was being followed...felt 13. was felt 14. died 15. is influenced 16. was stolen...was caught

◇ **7 (p. 79):** 1. Rice is grown in India. 2. This rug was made by my aunt. 3. My car is being fixed today. 4. French is spoken in Quebec. 5. That bridge was designed by Mr. Eads in the 1870s. 6. The wheel was invented thousands of years ago. 7. Was the telephone invented by Thomas Edison? 8. A new hospital is going to be built just outside of town. 9. How are candles made? 10. That TV show is watched by very few people. 11. Look! The seals are being fed.

◇ 9 (p. 81): 1. (I.O. = Jack) Jack is going to be served breakfast in bed on his birthday.   2. (I.O. = Mike) Mike has been offered the opportunity to study abroad.   3. (I.O. = babysitters) Babysitters aren't paid a lot of money.   4. (I.O. = me) When I was living in Kuwait, I was taught Arabic by my neighbor.   5. (I.O. = Jason) Jason was awarded a medal for distinguished service in the military.   6. (I.O. = you) You will be sent a copy of the sales contract by the real estate office.   7. (I.O. = me) I was handed a telegram when I answered the door.   8. (I.O. = the schoolchildren) The schoolchildren are going to be given a special tour of the modern art exhibit by the director of the museum, Ms. Cynthia Hall.   9. (I.O = Mr. French) Mr. French was given a gold watch upon his retirement from the company.

◇ 10 (p. 81): 1. will be told   2. completed   3. was assisted   4. was being ignored (*also possible*: had been ignored)   5. did you buy...didn't buy...was given.... Do you like   6. applied ...was hired   7. lie...are fed   8. will probably be eroded (OR: is probably going to be eroded)   9. had already been rented   10. were introduced...were eaten...are exported ...are enjoyed   11. is going to be interviewed (OR: will be interviewed)...has collected   12. is circled...are held...are circled   13. worshiped (*alternative spelling:* worshipped)

◇ 12 (p. 84): 1. redecorated   2. threading   3. smuggled   4. dragged   5. exposed   6. scrubbing   7. wound   8. broadcast   9. shoved   10. financed   11. leaning   12. mined   13. stretched   14. bred

◇ 14 (p. 85): 1. Pandas should be saved from extinction.   2. All traffic laws must be obeyed.   3. This broken window ought to be repaired.   4. The hotel guests should have been supplied with clean towels.   5. This garbage had better be taken to the dump soon.   6. Tomatoes can be picked before they are completely ripe.   7. The profits are supposed to be divided among the shareholders.   8. Bob's feelings must have been hurt.   9. This work has to be finished today.   10. The accident ought to have been reported to the police.   11. Bananas shouldn't be put in the freezer.

◇ 15 (p. 86): 1. be told   2. repeated   3. be wrapped   4. forgotten   5. been discovered   6. sew   7. been replaced   8. cost   9. whisper   10. be polluted   11. be considered   12. be worn   13. be signed   14. read

◇ 17 (p. 89): 1. are excited   2. are covered   3. is cracked   4. are exhausted   5. Are...finished   6. was insured   7. is polluted   8. is closed   9. is stuck   10. is dressed   11. am ...confused   12. are buried

◇ 19 (p. 91): 1. about   2. with   3. for   4. to   5. with   6. against   7. to   8. with   9. in   10. with   11. to   12. to   13. of   14. with   15. of   16. with   17. to...in   18. in...with   19. to...of

◇ 20 (p. 91): 1. with   2. for   3. from   4. with   5. in   6. to   7. to   8. with   9. with   10. with   11. of   12. to   13. with   14. to   15. for   16. with   17. in...to... with   18. with...in...to

◇ 22 (p. 93): 1. got torn   2. get broken   3. got lost   4. get hired   5. get hurt   6. was getting worried   7. got...soaked   8. get started   9. got buried   10. got stuck

◇ 24 (p. 95): 1. (a) interesting (b) interested   2. (a) irritating (b) irritated   3. (a) tired (b) tiring   4. (a) boiling (b) boiled   5. (a) upset (b) upsetting   6. (a) confusing (b) confused   7. (a) disappointing (b) disappointed   8. (a) reassuring (b) reassured   9. (a) frustrating (b) frustrated   10. (a) disturbing (b) disturbed   11. (a) convincing (b) convinced   12. (a) moving (b) moved   13. (a) shocking (b) shocked   14. (a) depressed (b) depressing   15. (a) humiliated (b) humiliating   16. (a) intriguing (b) intrigued

◇ **25 (p. 96):** 1. Polluted   2. furnished   3. dividing   4. running   5. invited   6. elected   7. suggested   8. written   9. exhausting   10. stimulating   11. spoken   12. falling   13. Frozen   14. invading   15. thrilling

◇ **28 (p. 100):** 1. The children were **frightened** by....
2. Two people got **hurt** in the accident and were **taken** to....
3. The movie was so **boring** that....
4. The students **were** helped by....
5. That allloy is **composed of** iron and tin.
6. The winner of the race hasn't been **announced** yet.
7. If you are **interested** in....   It is **fascinating.**
8. Progress is **being** made every day.
9. When, where, and by whom **was** the automobile **invented?**
10. ... have always been **interested** in learning....
11. I **do** not agree with ... think you'll **ever convince** me.
12. ... it is **accompanied** by....
13. Arthur was **given** an award by....
14. ... I was getting very **worried** about my son.
15. The problem was very **puzzling.** I couldn't figure it out.
16. Many strange **things happened** last night.

◇ **PRACTICE TEST A (p. 101):** 1. A   2. C   3. A   4. C   5. D   6. D   7. C   8. D   9. C   10. B   11. A   12. C   13. B   14. D   15. B   16. C   17. A   18. B   19. D   20. A

Chapter 4: GERUNDS AND INFINITIVES

◇ **1 (p. 105):** 1. of asking   2. to seeing   3. of washing   4. for breaking   5. from opening   6. of talking   7. like having   8. to killing   9. about finishing   10. for locking ... (for) making   11. of practicing

◇ **4 (p. 106):** 1. B   2. B   3. A   4. A   5. B   6. B   7. A   8. B   9. B   10. A   11. B   12. A   13. A   14. A   15. B   16. B   17. B   18. B   19. A   20. A

◇ **5 (p. 107):** 1. asked Jim to give   2. were warned not to park   3. reminded him to brush   4. are required to wear   5. advised me to consult   6. was ordered to leave   7. are expected to complete   8. reminded my husband to buy   9. advised me to get   10. were warned not to be   11. is permitted to use   12. asked her father to buy   13. encouraged our grandfather to write   14. was ordered not to shout

◇ **7 (p. 109):** 1. B   2. A, B   3. A, B   4. A, B   5. A, B   6. B   7. A, B   8. B   9. A, B   10. A, B   11. A   12. B   13. A, B   14. A, B   15. B   16. A   17. B   18. A   19. B   20. A   21. A   22. B   23. A   24. B   25. A   26. B

◇ **9 (p. 111):** (The answers are included in the Practice.)

◇ **10 (p. 111):** 1. to refund   2. to be   3. to buy   4. throwing   5. to get   6. to wear   7. to visit   8. to be   9. thinking   10. to attend   11. to leave   12. to cut   13. to ignore   14. singing   15. avoiding   16. to count   17. painting   18. to get   19. paying   20. to keep   21. taking   22. to know   23. moving   24. to watch   25. to keep

◇ **11 (p. 113):** 1. to operate   2. to shoot   3. having   4. to go   5. getting   6. to attend   7. to come   8. to turn   9. to tell   10. practicing   11. to clean   12. reading   13. sending   14. to see   15. to go   16. taking   17. to speak   18. receiving   19. to meet   20. getting   21. staying   22. to apologize   23. to obey   24. seeing   25. to take

◇ **12 (p. 114):** 1. A   2. B   3. A   4. A   5. B   6. A   7. B   8. B   9. A   10. A   11. B   12. B   13. A   14. B   15. B

◇ **16 (p. 116):** 1. in order   2. ∅   3. ∅   4. in order   5. ∅   6. in order   7. in order   8. in order   9. ∅   10. in order   11. in order   12. ∅   13. in order   14. in order   15. in order   16. ∅   17. in order   18. ∅

◇ **18 (p. 117):** 1. very   2. too   3. too   4. very   5. too   6. too   7. very   8. too   9. very   10. very   11. very...too   12. too   13. very   14. too   15. too

◇ **19 (p. 118):** 1. B   2. B   3. A   4. B   5. B   6. B   7. B   8. A   9. B   10. B

◇ **20 (p. 119):** 1. B   2. A   3. B   4. B   5. A   6. B   7. B   8. B   9. A   10. B

◇ **21 (p. 119):** 1. B   2. D   3. A   4. C   5. B   6. A   7. B   8. C   9. B   10. D   11. A   12. A   13. B   14. B   15. D

◇ **22 (p. 120):** 1. B   2. C   3. D   4. D   5. C   6. D   7. B   8. B   9. A   10. A

◇ **23 (p. 121):**
1. My mother was angry about **my losing** (OR: **having lost**) my new watch.
2. We look forward to **their spending** their vacation with us.
3. No one can understand **Tony's failing** (OR: **having failed**) the economics test even though....
4. I am upset about the **students' being required** to pay an extra fee to use the laboratory.
5. The supervisor appreciated **Mary's working** (OR: **having worked**) late to finish the project.
6. I will no longer tolerate **your being** late to work every morning.

◇ **24 (p. 121):** 1. D   2. A   3. C   4. A   5. A   6. D   7. B   8. C   9. D   10. B   11. D   12. C   13. B   14. C   15. A

◇ **26 (p. 123):** 1. practice   2. open   3. prevent   4. win   5. snoring   6. arrive   7. emerge (*also possible:* emerging)   8. perform (*also possible:* performing)   9. climb (*also possible:* climbing)   10. chirp (*also possible:* chirping)   11. explain   12. melt

◇ **28 (p. 124):** 1. C   2. A, B   3. A   4. A   5. C   6. B   7. A   8. A, B   9. A   10. A

◇ **31 (p. 125):** 1. B   2. A   3. B   4. C   5. C   6. D   7. D   8. B   9. B   10. C   11. B   12. A   13. A   14. C   15. D   16. D   17. D   18. B   19. D   20. C

◇ **32 (p. 127):** 1. to buy   2. opening   3. being asked   4. having   5. to wear...dressing   6. being allowed   7. jumping...falling   8. being taken   9. Observing...climb (OR: climbing)...realize   10. to stop delivering...to fill   11. gazing...(in order) to cheer   12. to have been performed   13. wash...come   14. having   15. being surprised (OR: having been surprised)...planning   16. being   17. to move   18. to help...resolve (OR: to resolve)...not to interfere   19. to be identified   20. to apply   21. to learn...to discover...promoting   22. reminding...to lock...trying to remember   23. to pick   24. meeting (OR: having met)...to be introduced   25. asking...forgetting   26. to be considered (OR: to have been considered)   27. not to sign   28. to sleep...thinking   29. notifying...to call   30. burning...coming

◇ **34 (p. 132):**   1. Please promise not **to tell** anybody....
2. I would appreciate **hearing** from you soon.
3. ...let very young **children stay** at home alone.
4. ...complained about **having** a handicap.
5. Mr. Lee didn't remember **to** bring his passport....
6. Lillian deserves to be **told** the truth....
7. Ali **doesn't** speak Spanish, and Juan **doesn't** know Arabic. But they communicate well by **speaking** English when they **are** together.
8. I enjoyed **talking** to her....   I look forward to **seeing** her next week.
9. ...everyone is required **to leave** the building.
10. **Attending** the premiere of the new....
11. Don't keep **asking** me the same....
12. I anticipate **arriving** at the airport....
13. Let **me help** you **carry** that table upstairs.
14. ...I found my young son **standing** on....

◇ **PRACTICE TEST A (p. 134):**   1. A   2. B   3. D   4. A   5. B   6. D   7. C   8. D   9. D
10. A   11. B   12. D   13. B   14. B   15. C   16. C   17. D
18. C   19. A   20. B

Appendix 1:   SUPPLEMENTARY GRAMMAR UNITS

◇ **1 (p. 137):**

SUBJECT	VERB	OBJECT
1. politician	supported	taxes
2. mechanic	repaired	engine
3. boxes	contain	photographs
4. teacher	canceled......	test
5. earthquake ..	destroyed.....	village
6. birds	have..........	feathers

List of all of the nouns: politician, taxes, mechanic, engine, boxes, photographs, teacher, test, earthquake, village, birds, feathers.

◇ **2 (p. 137):**   1. repeated (**VT**)   2. rises (**VI**)   3. divided (**VT**)   4. sneezed (**VI**)   5. happened (**VI**)
6. bought (**VT**)   7. won (**VT**)   8. won (**VI**)   9. arrived (**VI**)   10. waited (**VI**)
11. are staying (**VI**)   12. is blowing (**VI**)   13. agree (**VI**)   14. walked (**VI**)...rode (**VT**)

◇ **3 (p. 138):**

PREPOSITION	OBJECT OF PREPOSITION
1. in..............	field
2. from	table
3. in..............	garage
4. during	storm
5. on	horses
for.............	transportation
6. to.............	park
after	class

◇ **4 (p. 138):**

1. <u>Alex</u> <u>needs</u> new <u>batteries</u> <u>for his camera.</u>
    S   VT   O   PP

2. A <u>bomb</u> <u>exploded</u> <u>in the road.</u>
   S VI   PP

3. <u>Sally</u> <u>wore</u> her blue <u>suit</u> <u>to the meeting.</u>
   S   VT   O   PP

    S   **VI**   **PP**   **PP**
4. Jim came to class without his books.

    S   **VI**   **PP**
5. Dark clouds appeared on the horizon.

    S   **VT**   **O**   **PP**
6. Plants need a reliable supply of water.

    S   **VT**   **O**   **PP**   **PP**   **PP**
7. Mary filled the shelves of the cabinet with boxes of old books.

    S   **VT**   **O**   **PP**   **PP**   **PP**
8. We enjoyed the view of snowy mountains from the window of our hotel room.

    S   **VI**   **PP**   **PP**
9. The child sat between her parents on the sandy beach.

    PP   **S**   **VI**   **PP**
Above her, an eagle flew across the cloudless sky.

◇ **5 (p. 138):**

    ADJ   **ADV**   **ADJ**
1. A terrible fire spread rapidly through the old house.

    ADJ   **ADV**   **ADJ**
2. A small child cried noisily in the third row of the theater.

    ADJ   **ADV**
3. The eager player waited impatiently for the start of the game.

    ADV   **ADJ**
4. An unusually large crowd came to the concert.

    ADV   **ADJ**   **ADJ**
5. Arthur carefully repaired the antique vase with special glue.

    ADV   **ADJ**   **ADJ**   **ADV**
6. On especially busy days, the telephone in the main office rings constantly.

Total number of nouns: 16. *Total number of verbs:* 6.

◇ **6 (p. 139):**   1. quickly   2. quick   3. polite   4. politely   5. regularly   6. regular   7. usual   8. usually   9. well   10. good   11. gentle   12. gently   13. annually   14. annual   15. bad   16. badly

◇ **7 (p. 139):**
1. Sue **always takes** a walk in the morning.
2. Tim **is always** a hard worker.
3. Beth **has always worked** hard.
4. Jack **always works** hard.
5. **Do you always work** hard?
6. Taxis **are usually** available . . . .
7. Tom **rarely takes** a taxi . . . .
8. I **have often thought** about . . . .
9. Cindy **probably needs** some help.
10. **Have you ever attended** the show . . . ?
11. Al **seldom goes** out . . . .
12. The students **are hardly ever** late.
13. **Do you usually finish** your . . . ?
14. In India, the monsoon season **generally begins** in April.
15. . . . Mr. Singh's hometown **usually receives** around . . . .

◇ **8 (p. 140):**

LINKING VERB + ADJECTIVE	LINKING VERB + ADJECTIVE
1. Ø *(no linking verb in the sentence)*	7. Ø
2. looked . . . . fresh	8. Ø
3. Ø	9. Ø
4. Ø	10. smells . . . . delicious
5. tasted . . . . good	11. Ø
6. grew . . . . quiet	12. got . . . . sleepy

13. became . . . . rough   18. Ø
14. Ø   19. Ø
15. Ø   20. appears . . . . certain
16. sounded . . . . . . happy   21. seems . . . . strange
17. turns . . . . hot

◇ **9 (p. 140):**   1. clean   2. slowly   3. safely   4. anxious   5. complete   6. wildly   7. honest
8. thoughtfully   9. well   10. fair   11. terrible   12. good   13. light
14. confidently   15. famous   16. fine

◇ **11 (p. 142):**   1. them   2. me   3. I   4. me . . . his   5. his . . . her   6. its . . . them   7. They . . . it
8. your . . . them   9. I . . . him . . . me   10. My . . . I . . . . She . . . her . . . mine   11. Our
. . . our . . . ours . . . theirs   12. It . . . its . . . its . . . it . . . it . . . it . . . It's . . . them

◇ **12 (p. 142):**
1. . . . but I don't like most of **it**.
2. . . . my sister and **I** used to play . . . .
3. . . . study very hard for **them**.
4. . . . by my boss and **me** after . . . .
5. . . . most of **its** time . . . .
6. . . . so I've forgotten a lot of **it**.
7. . . . but I couldn't find **them**.
8. . . . speak to Tim and **me** about . . . . He explained **them** to . . . and asked for **our** opinions.
9. My father and **she** had come . . . . was waiting for **us** . . . .
10. . . . respect other people. **He** (OR: **She, S/he, He or she**) needs to . . . including **his** (OR: **her, his or her**) playmates. [NOTE: *The masculine-feminine pronoun problem can be avoided by using a plural noun:* **Children** should learn to respect . . . . **They** need . . . **their** playmates.]
11. . . . because **theirs** was in the garage . . . .

◇ **13 (p. 143):**   1. He's   2. Ø   3. He's   4. Ø   5. She'd   6. Ø   7. She'd   8. Ø   9. We'll
10. They're   11. It's   12. It's   13. Ø   14. Ø   15. We're   16. Ø   17. She's
18. She'd   19. She'd . . . we'd   20. Ø . . . he'd

◇ **14 (p. 144):**

	Question word	Auxiliary verb	Subject	Main verb	Rest of question
1a.	Ø	**Can**	Bob	**live**	there?
1b.	Where	**can**	Bob	**live**	Ø ?
1c.	Who	**can**	Ø	**live**	there?
2a.	Ø	**Is**	Don	**living**	there?
2b.	Where	**is**	Don	**living**	Ø ?
2c.	Who	**is**	Ø	**living**	there?
3a.	Ø	**Does**	Sue	**live**	there?
3b.	Where	**does**	**Sue**	**live**	Ø ?
3c.	Who	Ø	Ø	**lives**	there?
4a.	Ø	**Will**	Ann	**live**	there?
4b.	Where	**will**	**Ann**	**live**	Ø ?
4c.	Who	**will**	Ø	**live**	there?
5a.	Ø	**Did**	Jack	**live**	there?
5b.	**Where**	**did**	**Jack**	**live**	Ø ?
5c.	**Who**	Ø	Ø	**lived**	there?
6a.	Ø	**Has**	**Mary**	**lived**	**there?**
6b.	**Where**	**has**	**Mary**	**lived**	Ø ?
6c.	**Who**	**has**	Ø	**lived**	**there?**

◇ **15 (p. 145):**   1. When are you going to the zoo?   2. Are you going downtown later today?   3. Do you live in an apartment?   4. Where does Sue live?   5. Who lives in that house?   6. Can you speak French?   7. Who can speak Arabic?   8. When did Olga arrive?   9. Who arrived late?   10. What is Ann opening?   11. What is Ann doing?   12. What did Mary open? 13. Who opened the door?   14. Has the mail arrived?   15. Do you have a bicycle? 16. What does Alex have in his hand?   17. Do you like ice cream?   18. Would you like an ice cream cone?   19. What would Joe like?   20. Who would like a soft drink?

◇ **16 (p. 146):**   1. How long has Pierre been living here?   2. Which (city) is farther north, London or Paris?   3. Whose is it?   4. What have you been doing?   5. Who answered the phone? 6. How do they plow their fields?   7. How long have you had it?   8. What kind of bird is that?   9. Why were you late for work this morning? (OR: How come you were late for work this morning?)   10. How long did it take you?   11. What time/When did he finally get home?   12. How do you take it?   13. What is the population of the United States? 14. Which (coat/one) do you like better (, the red one or the black one)?   15. How did you get there?   16. Who(m) should I address it to? (*Formal:* To whom should I address it?) 17. How far (How many miles) is it from here to Los Angeles?   18. Who is going to be at the meeting tonight?   19. How often (How many times a week) do people in your country have rice?   20. Where did you get that silly looking hat?   21. How many edges are there on a cube?   ....   How many edges are there on a pyramid?   22. What does "apologize" mean?   23. What does he look like?   24. What is she like?

◇ **22 (p. 151):**   1. Haven't you seen...? No   2. Didn't he say...? Yes   3. Wasn't he...? No 4. Didn't Mary tell...? No   5. Aren't you having...? No   6. Don't Janet and you work ...? Yes   7. Isn't that...? Yes   8. Isn't the Mississippi...? No

◇ **23 (p. 152):**   1. don't you   2. have you   3. didn't she   4. aren't there   5. have you   6. don't you (*possible but less common:* haven't you)   7. won't you   8. doesn't he   9. shouldn't we 10. can they   11. are they   12. isn't it   13. did they   14. aren't I/am I not 15. isn't it

◇ **24 (p. 153):**   1. no...not   2. no...not   3. No   4. no   5. not...not   6. no   7. not 8. no   9. no...no   10. not   11. no   12. not

◇ **25 (p. 153):**   1. We **have no** time to waste. OR: We **don't have any** time to waste.   2. I **didn't have any** problems. OR: I **had no** problems.   3. I **can't do anything** about it. OR: I **can do nothing** about it.   4. You **can hardly ever understand** her when she speaks.   5. I **know neither** Ann **nor** her husband. OR: I **don't know either** Ann **or** her husband.   6. **Don't ever drink** water from.... OR: **Never drink** water from....   7. ...I **could barely hear** the speaker.

◇ **26 (p. 154):**   1. **Hardly had I stepped** out of bed....   2. **Never will I say** that again.   3. **Scarcely ever have I enjoyed** myself more....   4. **Rarely does she make** a mistake.   5. **Never will I trust** him again because....   6. **Hardly ever is it** possible to get....   7. **Seldom do I skip** breakfast.   8. **Never have I known** a more....

◇ **27 (p. 154):**   1. Ø Lightning...a flash...Ø thunder   2. **a** terrible storm...**the** thunder   3. Ø Circles ...Ø round geometric figures   4. **A** circle...**a** slash...**the** circle...**the** illustration 5. **The** milk...**the** refrigerator   6. Ø Milk...Ø protein...Ø calcium   7. Ø space...Ø other...**the** universe   8. **a** new phone   9. **the** phone   10. Ø Wisdom...Ø understanding ...Ø knowledge   11. **the** wisdom   12. **The** woman...**the** right answer...**the** teacher's question   13. **an** independent young woman   14. **a** car...**the** second day...**the** car 15. Ø People...Ø plants...Ø many different ways...Ø oxygen...Ø lifesaving medicines...Ø houses...Ø paper...Ø textiles.